MAGIC WITH LEFTOVERS

MAGIC WITH LEFTOVERS

LOUSENE ROUSSEAU
BRUNNER

Illustrated by PAUL CALLE

DOLPHIN BOOKS
DOUBLEDAY & COMPANY, INC.
GARDEN CITY, NEW YORK

CONTENTS

PREFACE

Rare indeed is the housewife who is never faced with the problem of making use of leftover foods—not merely the roast of beef, the leg of lamb, the baked ham, the roast turkey, but the innumerable odds and ends: a cupful of mashed potato, three ears of green corn, a couple of frankfurters, a bowl of rice, two egg whites, half a loaf of stale bread, or an endless assortment of other items.

This cookbook, devoted wholly to using up leftovers, has grown out of long experience in my own kitchen, where for a number of years a good part of my cooking has been for just two people. Because I was not willing to do without large juicy roasts, big thick steaks, large fat turkeys and chickens, baked hams, and the like, I learned how to make really inviting new dishes out of the leftovers. *Magic with Leftovers* contains three hundred recipes of this sort, many of them so good that we prefer them to the originals. They cover a wide variety of *kinds* of dishes: cocktail canapés, appetizers, soups, sandwiches, main dishes for luncheon and dinner, salads, vegetables, and a few desserts. The meat and poultry recipes include ways of using leftovers at all stages: whole slices, diced, chopped, and ground. I have organized them according to the principal leftover ingredient, but the detailed index lists every recipe using that ingredient. Leftover rice, for example, is used in a number of meat and vegetable recipes.

A little ingenuity goes a long way in making cooking with leftovers interesting, challenging, and economical. Experienced cooks know that you can take great liberties with recipes using leftovers, omitting some ingredients and adding others that happen to be on hand. Skimpy amounts of one item can be pieced out with something else. Ham can be added to many beef, veal, and chicken recipes, and most pork recipes. A pair of sweetbreads will stretch leftover chicken and add to its flavor. A small can of chicken will sometimes make the difference between enough leftover chicken for a recipe and not enough. A can of breakfast sausages cut up will stretch many meat dishes. Most fish and seafood recipes are even improved by adding a can of another seafood—crabmeat, lobster, or shrimp.

The thrifty cook never throws away leftovers. A tablespoon of many vegetables can be added to vegetable or cream soups. A strip of bacon can be crumbled into a one-egg muffin recipe, or blended with a little cream cheese for a sandwich or canapé spread. A bit of gravy can be added to soups or to the consommé or chicken broth called for in many recipes.

Planning ahead for leftovers often saves a good deal of work in preparing meals. Thus a larger chicken or fish than your family needs will mean enough left for a delectable casserole two or three days later. An extra half cup of rice boiled will provide enough left over to make the basis of another main dish. Usually, a good-sized roast not only is juicier and better, but gives you the makings of two or three more meals. An extra lobster boiled will make a fine salad or casserole. An extra-large mess of shrimps can be used up in a number of fine dishes. An extra half-dozen ears of corn can be used to wonderful advantage.

A deep freezer is a priceless asset in leftover cookery, because it lets you delay the reappearance of food as long as you please. When you freeze large amounts of leftover roasts, turkey, and the like, cut into meal-sized portions, you can thaw out just enough for one dish. Or with a frozen-food saw you can saw off just what you need for a dish without thawing the rest. Never refreeze thawed food.

One caution is important in leftover cookery, particularly with meat. With very few exceptions, meat once cooked must not be recooked for more than the shortest possible time, often just long enough to heat it through well. Overcooking makes it dry and tasteless.

A final word about leftovers is in order: it is by no means always advisable to make new dishes out of all leftovers. Many baked or roasted meats and poultry are delicious merely sliced and served cold. Some can even be reheated to advantage. In that case, slice it first, wrap loosely but securely (no cracks) in aluminum foil, lay in a shallow casserole or pie plate, and heat about fifteen minutes in a moderate oven. Leftover boiled rice put in a sieve or colander and steamed ten minutes over boiling water can hardly be told from freshly cooked rice. Many vegetables and creamed dishes can be reheated in a double boiler—not over direct heat—without loss of flavor. Mashed potatoes can be spread in a greased pyrex plate, dotted generously with butter and a dash of paprika, and heated fifteen minutes in a moderate oven. And so on endlessly.

But when you do want a "new look" with your leftovers, I hope the recipes in this book will give you plenty of variety and flavor.

Note: "Leftover" is abbreviated to "LO" in the list of ingredients for each recipe.

MEATS

MEATS

BEEF

BAKED BEEF ROLL

2 cups LO* pot roast or roast beef	1 cup rich cream sauce
	salt and pepper
1 cup mixed cooked vegetables	biscuit dough
	melted butter
1 small onion	1 egg yolk
1 cup mushrooms	

Here is a dish that is both interesting looking and interesting tasting.

Put meat, vegetables, onion, and mushrooms through the food chopper, using medium blade. Stir in cream sauce made with 2 tablespoons butter or margarine, 2 tablespoons flour, and 1 cup top milk. Season to taste. Let this mixture stand while you make biscuit dough. Use your favorite recipe, but add a little "zip" to it by sifting 1 teaspoon curry powder with flour and baking powder, and moisten with white wine instead of milk. Roll or pat out into a rectangle ¼–⅛ inch thick, rolling on floured waxed paper. Spread the meat mixture gently on biscuit dough, covering it evenly except for the ends. Roll up like a jelly roll, lifting the waxed paper as you roll to avoid breaking up the biscuit part. Moisten dough at the ends and pinch together. Slide the roll onto a baking sheet with the seam down. Bake in a hot oven, 425°, 30–35 minutes. After 15 minutes brush crust with melted butter, and in another 10 minutes brush with beaten yolk of egg. Serve with tomato or mushroom sauce. Slice as you would a jelly roll.   SERVES 6.

* Leftover.

BEEF (OR LAMB) BONNE FEMME

2 cups LO beef or lamb, diced small
1 tablespoon bacon fat or butter
2 tablespoons chopped onion
1 tablespoon flour
1½ cups consommé
3 tablespoons tomato purée or tomato sauce or soup
1 tablespoon chopped parsley
2 cups fresh hot mashed potatoes
grated Parmesan cheese
2 tablespoons fine bread crumbs
1 tablespoon butter

This is an interesting variation of one type of Shepherd's Pie, featured by tomato flavoring and cheese topping.

Sauté onion lightly in fat in heavy skillet. Blend in flour and cook a moment. Gradually add consommé and tomato purée, stirring constantly until smooth and thickened. Stir in parsley and meat, bring just to a boil, and pour in 6-cup casserole. Spread potatoes on top, sprinkle generously with Parmesan cheese and bread crumbs, add butter in little dabs, and either brown under broiler or heat in a hot oven, 450°, about 10 minutes, or until top is well browned.

SERVES 4–5.

BEEF MENAGÈRE

2 cups LO roast beef, diced rather small
4 tablespoons butter or margarine
3 medium potatoes peeled and diced or chopped very fine
salt and pepper
1 small onion chopped
2 tablespoons tomato purée or tomato sauce
¾ cup LO gravy thinned with a little dry red wine or consommé
1 tablespoon chopped parsley

Accompanied by broiled tomato halves, this dish makes a good meal, simply prepared.

Heat 3 tablespoons of the butter or margarine in a heavy skillet and sauté potatoes in it, stirring frequently to brown well. Season to taste. While they are cooking, melt remaining butter in another skillet and sauté onion lightly. Stir in tomato purée, gravy, parsley, and meat, and heat to boiling, stirring frequently. Season to taste and stir in about half of the browned potatoes. Pour in hot serving dish, top with remaining potatoes, and serve at once.   SERVES 4.

BEEF-EGGPLANT CASSEROLE

2–3 *cups LO beef chopped*
1 *medium eggplant cut in*
    ½-inch slices
2 *tablespoons grated onion*
1 *small clove garlic mashed*
2 *tablespoons parsley*
salt and pepper

pinch nutmeg
½ *teaspoon marjoram*
3 *tablespoons olive oil*
1 *cup tomato sauce*
    (canned) or 1 can con-
    densed tomato soup

Eggplant combines wonderfully in casseroles, both with beef and with lamb. This is a very good one with beef, and simple.

Fix the eggplant first. An easy way to get rid of its slightly bitter taste is to salt the slices well (do not peel), pile on top of each other in the shape of the original eggplant, and put a moderate weight, such as a bowl, on top. Let stand 20–30 minutes.

Mix meat with onion, garlic, parsley, salt and pepper to taste, nutmeg, and marjoram. Let it stand while you brown eggplant slices (cut in quarters first) in olive oil. Grease a medium casserole and arrange alternate layers of meat mixture and eggplant, adding a tablespoon of tomato sauce to each eggplant layer. Pour remaining sauce over the top. Bake in a 375° oven 20 minutes.   SERVES 5–6.

BEEF FERMIÈRE

thin slices of LO roast beef
2 tablespoons bacon fat,
    butter, or margarine
1 cup chopped onions
1 tablespoon flour
1 cup consommé

½ cup tomato purée or
    tomato sauce
salt and pepper
bread crumbs
1 tablespoon butter

Lay slices of beef on a heat-proof platter, overlapping them.
Melt fat in skillet and sauté onions until they begin to
brown, stirring frequently. Blend in flour and cook until
smooth. Add consommé and tomato purée, stirring constantly until thickened. Season to taste and pour over sliced
meat. Sprinkle with crumbs, dot with butter, and brown
10 minutes in hot oven, 450°, or under broiler.

BEEF IN HORSERADISH SAUCE

3 cups LO roast beef cut in
    1-inch dice
2 tablespoons bacon fat or
    butter
1 medium onion sliced thin
½ teaspoon curry powder
¼ teaspoon ground ginger
½ teaspoon sugar
2 teaspoons Worcestershire
    sauce

½ teaspoon salt
½ teaspoon pepper
1 cup thinned beef gravy,
    consommé, or half
    consommé and half red
    wine
1 cup sour cream
1 tablespoon prepared
    horseradish
1 teaspoon minced parsley

This is a very simple dish to make, and it is so good that
it makes one grateful for leftover beef.

Brown beef lightly in sizzling fat. Transfer to casserole
and arrange onions on top. Remove skillet from stove, add
curry powder, ginger, sugar, Worcestershire, salt and pepper, and gravy. Blend well and pour over casserole. Cover
and simmer in moderate oven, 300°, 35–40 minutes. Just

before serving stir in sour cream and horseradish. Sprinkle with parsley and serve at once, with hot fluffy rice or buttered noodles.   SERVES 6.

Note: If you prefer a thicker gravy, thicken with flour and water paste 5 minutes before serving.

BEEF PANCAKE CASSEROLE

1 *cup LO beef chopped fine*
1 *cup prepared pancake
    mix*
1½ *cups milk*
4 *tablespoons melted butter*
1 *well-beaten egg*
2 *tablespoons finely
    chopped onion*

bacon fat
salt and pepper
2 *tablespoons minced
    parsley*
½ *cup sour cream*
2 *tablespoons grated
    Parmesan cheese*

A simple, inexpensive, and easily prepared dish, especially good for a hearty luncheon or for Sunday night supper.

Add milk to pancake flour, stir in 1 tablespoon melted butter and the egg, beat well, and let stand while you prepare the meat. Brown onion lightly in 1 tablespoon bacon fat, stir in chopped beef and let it cook a moment, season to taste, and add to pancake batter.

Cook pancakes in bacon fat on a hot griddle or in a heavy skillet, making them quite large. As each one is finished sprinkle it with a little parsley, roll up, and lay in a shallow well-greased casserole, packing closely together. Keep casserole in a warm oven until the last pancake is made and then turn heat up to 350°. Spread rolls with remaining melted butter, sour cream, and Parmesan cheese. Put in oven until cheese is melted, about 10 minutes, and then under the broiler a moment to brown cheese.   SERVES 4.

BEEF PARMENTIER

3 cups LO beef diced
5 tablespoons butter or
   margarine
2 cups potatoes peeled and
   diced very small

salt and pepper
1 tablespoon chopped
   parsley

Here is an extremely simple recipe to make leftover beef palatable.

Heat 3 tablespoons of the butter in a heavy skillet and brown potatoes to golden, stirring frequently to brown evenly. Salt to taste. When they are tender remove to bowl and keep warm. Heat remaining 2 tablespoons butter in same skillet and quickly brown meat over a brisk flame, stirring constantly. Season to taste, put back the potatoes, shake all together, put in serving dish and sprinkle top with parsley.   SERVES 6.

BREADED SLICES OF BEEF

LO roast or boiled beef
   sliced ¼ inch thick
salt and pepper
minced parsley
vinegar
flour

1 egg
2 tablespoons milk
1 tablespoon salad oil
fine dry bread crumbs
butter or bacon fat

Spread out slices of beef, season lightly, and sprinkle each slice with parsley and a few drops of vinegar. Let stand 15–30 minutes. Put flour in one flat soup plate, egg, milk, and salad oil in another, mixed just enough to blend well, and bread crumbs in a third. Dip slices of beef in flour, then in egg, and then in bread crumbs. Let stand 15–20 minutes to dry the crust a little. Heat fat to sizzling in heavy skillet and sauté slices to rich golden brown on both sides. Serve with tomato sauce or leftover beef gravy thinned with a little consommé or red wine.

CHILI-CORN PIE

2 cups LO beef ground
    coarsely
4 strips bacon ground
2 tablespoons bacon fat
1 large onion sliced
½ cup seedless raisins

¾ cup sliced stuffed olives
1 cup whole-kernel corn—
    fresh, frozen, canned, or
    cut off LO boiled cobs
salt and pepper
1 tablespoon butter

Put the leftover beef and the bacon through the meat grinder together. Melt bacon fat in skillet and lightly brown onions. Add meat and sauté over high heat just enough to brown a bit. Season to taste. In a small casserole make alternate layers of meat mixture, raisins, and olives, making 2 layers of each. Spread corn in a thick layer on top, season lightly, dot with butter, and bake 20 minutes in moderate oven, 350°. Cover the casserole for the first 10 minutes.

SERVES 4.

COLD ROAST BEEF SALAD

2 cups cold roast beef
    chopped or diced small
1 cup cooked potatoes
    diced small
½ cup cooked green beans
    cut in small pieces
½ cup cooked beets diced
    small
½ cup unpeeled radishes
    sliced thin

1 cup watercress leaves
    coarsely chopped
2 tablespoons chives cut
    fine
1 cup chili sauce
½ cup tarragon vinegar
dash Tabasco
salt to taste

Combine meat, vegetables, and herbs in a large bowl. Mix chili sauce, vinegar, Tabasco, and salt to taste. Pour over bowl and mix lightly but thoroughly. Chill well before serving. Arrange in large bowl lined with crisp lettuce leaves and garnish with wedges of ripe tomatoes.

SERVES 6.

COLD ROAST BEEF VINAIGRETTE

LO roast beef sliced thin
paper-thin slices of onion

Vinaigrette sauce:
- 1 *tablespoon vinegar*
- 4 *tablespoons olive oil*
- ¼ *teaspoon prepared*
  mustard
- 1 *teaspoon minced*
  parsley
- 1 *teaspoon tarragon,*
  chervil, and chives
  mixed

Arrange slices overlapping down center of platter, with a slice of onion on top of each slice of beef. Mix well the ingredients of the sauce and spoon out evenly over meat. On one side of platter arrange sliced tomatoes, seasoned and sprinkled with minced parsley and chives. On the other side arrange a mixed vegetable salad, made with such vegetables as LO lima beans, string beans, green peas, whole-kernel corn, and carrots, mixed with a few sliced unpeeled radishes and a little celery thinly sliced, tossed with a little French dressing, and blended with mayonnaise to which a little sour cream is added.

CREOLE BEEF

- 2 *cups LO beef diced small*
- 3 *tablespoons butter or*
  margarine
- 1 *tablespoon chopped green*
  pepper
- 1 *tablespoon chopped onion*
- 3 *tablespoons flour*
- 1½ *cups consommé*

- ½ *cup tomato purée or un-*
  diluted tomato soup
- *salt and pepper*
- ½ *teaspoon paprika*
- 1 *teaspoon lemon juice*
- ½ *teaspoon prepared horse-*
  radish well drained

Melt butter and cook green pepper and onion in it until soft but not brown. Blend in flour and gradually stir in consommé, tomato, and remaining ingredients, with salt and pepper to taste. When sauce is smooth and thickened add beef and heat through well. Serve in a border of rice.

SERVES 5–6.

HAMBURGER PINWHEELS

2 cups LO beef chopped fine
2 tablespoons bacon fat
1 medium onion chopped fine
½ teaspoon sweet basil
¼ teaspoon marjoram
½ teaspoon minced parsley
1 tablespoon flour
¾ cup milk
1 recipe biscuits

Melt fat in skillet, brown onion lightly, add meat, and brown quickly. Stir in herbs, sprinkle with flour, stir until it is absorbed, season to taste, and let simmer a few minutes. Add milk and stir until smooth. Remove from heat. Roll or pat your favorite biscuit dough on a pastry cloth or waxed paper, shaping it into a rectangle a little longer than it is wide, and about ⅜ inch thick. Spread meat mixture on the dough, leaving a little margin all around. Roll up the long way, lifting the cloth or waxed paper as you roll to help the soft dough roll smoothly. With a sharp greased knife cut the roll into slices about an inch wide, placing each as you cut it in a flat shallow casserole or oven-proof pie plate, well greased. Bake in a 375° oven about 30 minutes, or until brown. Serve with a rich cream sauce with a few leftover green peas added, or tomato sauce. SERVES 6.

QUICK MACARONI-HAMBURGER CASSEROLE

2 cups LO beef ground
3 cups cooked macaroni
4 tablespoons bacon fat or
   butter
1 large onion chopped
1 clove garlic mashed
1 green pepper chopped
1 can condensed tomato
   soup
½ can water
1½ teaspoons salt
1 teaspoon paprika

½ teaspoon oregano
½ teaspoon sweet basil
½ teaspoon minced parsley
1 teaspoon Worcestershire
   sauce
2 tablespoons catsup or
   tomato paste
2 teaspoons Angostura
   bitters
1 cup coarsely grated
   American or Cheddar
   cheese, firmly packed

This dish can be put together quickly, in spite of its many ingredients.

Melt fat in heavy skillet and sauté onion, garlic, and green pepper. As soon as they begin to color, add meat and brown lightly but quickly, stirring constantly. Mix soup and water and add to skillet with seasonings and herbs. In a greased 2-quart casserole put half the macaroni, then half the meat mixture, and a layer of cheese. (Take out 2 tablespoons of cheese for the top and use half the remainder for this layer.) Repeat layers, top with reserved cheese, cover, and bake in 375° oven for 35 minutes. Remove cover and bake an additional 10–15 minutes, or until top is browned.

SERVES 4–5.

MEXICAN CHILI

2 *cups LO beef coarsely* *ground*
1 *tablespoon bacon fat*
1 *medium onion chopped*
1 *medium green pepper chopped*
2 *cups canned tomatoes*

½ *can tomato paste*
1–2 *teaspoons chili powder*
salt and pepper
1 *teaspoon Worcestershire sauce*
1 *can kidney beans*

Make this dish as hot as you like, by increasing amount of chili powder.

Brown onion and green pepper lightly in bacon fat in small heavy soup kettle. Add tomatoes, tomato paste, and seasonings. Cover and simmer gently 45 minutes, stirring occasionally. Add meat and continue cooking 15 minutes more. Add kidney beans just before serving and allow to heat through. Serve with lots of fluffy rice or on spaghetti.

SERVES 5–6.

PAPRIKA BEEF

3 *cups LO beef diced small*
3 *tablespoons bacon fat*
½ *cup chopped onions*

2 *tablespoons paprika*
½ *cup cream*
½ *cup cream sauce*

The paprika flavor here gives a delightful flavor to the beef.

Heat fat in skillet and brown beef quickly, stirring or shaking pan constantly. Remove to a bowl, and in fat remaining in pan brown onions lightly, over medium heat. Mix paprika and cream and stir into onions. Add cream sauce (made with 2 teaspoons butter or margarine, 2 teaspoons flour, ½ cup milk, and salt to taste). Stir in meat and just heat well—*do not boil.*

SERVES 5–6.

ROAST BEEF HASH I

2½ cups finely diced or
    ground LO cooked beef
2 cups chopped or ground
    raw potato

1 medium onion grated or
    ground
1 cup consommé
2 tablespoons bacon fat
salt and pepper

An easy way to prepare this type of hash is to put everything through the food-chopper, using a medium blade:
beef, potato, and onion. Mix well with consommé, add salt
and pepper to taste. Heat fat to sizzling in heavy skillet,
turn in mixture, cover, reduce heat, and simmer over very
low heat about 25 minutes, or until lightly browned on the
under side. Uncover and place in moderate oven, 350°, for
15–20 minutes. Loosen with a spatula, fold over like an
omelet, and slide out on heated platter.   SERVES 5.

ROAST BEEF HASH II

2 cups LO cooked beef
    chopped or diced small
4 medium LO cooked
    potatoes cut in small
    dice

2 medium onions chopped
salt and pepper
beef gravy or milk
2 tablespoons bacon fat

This recipe is a handy one when you have both potatoes
and beef left over.

Mix beef, potatoes, and onions with a little thinned-out
gravy to moisten, or a little milk if you have no gravy.
Season to taste. Heat fat to sizzling in heavy skillet, turn
in hash, stir well, cover skillet, and cook over very low
heat until under side is a good brown. Fold over and slide onto
heated platter. Or, if you prefer, stir occasionally while hash
is browning and serve as a loose browned hash. SERVES 4–5.

ROAST BEEF HASH III

3–4 *cups LO roast beef*
2 *cups raw potatoes*
1 *large onion peeled*
1 *green pepper*
1 *cup dry red wine*

LO beef gravy if available
3 *tablespoons bacon fat*
1 *clove garlic mashed*
salt and pepper

Hash cooked in red wine has an especially delicious flavor.

Put beef, potatoes, onion, and green pepper in a large chopping bowl and chop together until rather finely minced, but it should not look as though it had been put through the meat grinder. Stir in the wine and up to ½ cup leftover gravy if you have it. Heat fat to sizzling in a large heavy skillet, brown garlic in it, turn in hash mixture, and cook over low flame until potatoes are tender. Stir several times while cooking and add salt and pepper to taste. If you want to serve it with a crisp brown crust, do not stir the last 15 minutes. When done, use a spatula to fold the hash over like an omelet, and slide out on a hot platter.

SERVES 6–8.

MEAT LOAF IN A LOAF

2 *cups LO roast beef*
   (*preferably rare*)
   minced
1 *fat loaf French bread,*
   Vienna type

1 *can evaporated milk*
1 *medium onion minced*
1 *green pepper minced*
1 *egg*
salt and pepper to taste

Cut a thin slice across the top of the loaf of bread and pull out most of the insides with a sharp-tined fork, leaving a shell an inch or less thick all round. Soak 2 cups of these pieces in the evaporated milk 10–15 minutes. Add remaining ingredients to the soaked bread, mix well, and pack rather firmly in the bread shell. Put back the cover, lay the loaf on a baking sheet, and bake in a 350° oven about 45 minutes. This loaf can be served either hot or cold. Slice right through the loaf—don't scoop out the meat. SERVES 6.

STEAK OR ROAST BEEF PIE

3 cups LO roast beef or
    steak cut in ¾-inch
    cubes
3 tablespoons bacon fat
1 clove garlic mashed
1 large onion sliced
¼ pound mushrooms sliced
3 tablespoons flour
2½ cups consommé

½ cup red wine
salt and pepper
1 teaspoon minced parsley
½ teaspoon marjoram
1 teaspoon Worcestershire
    sauce
pastry or biscuits for crust
2 tablespoons sherry (opt.)

Melt fat in heavy skillet and sauté garlic, onion, and mushrooms until onion begins to take on color. Stir in meat and
sauté lightly a few moments. Sprinkle flour over and mix
well. Pour on consommé and wine, stirring constantly until
sauce is smooth and thickened. Season to taste and add
herbs and Worcestershire sauce. Pour in 2-quart casserole
and top with either rolled pastry, slashed to allow steam
to escape, or small baking-powder biscuits. Bake in hot
oven, 450°, about 20 minutes, or until top is golden brown.
Before serving pour sherry into the pie through slits or between biscuits, using a small funnel.   SERVES 6.

STEAK AND KIDNEY PIE

2–3 cups LO steak or roast
    beef cut in ¾-inch cubes
2 veal kidneys or 4 lamb
    kidneys
2 tablespoons bacon fat or
    beef fat
1 large onion chopped
    coarsely

2 cups condensed
    consommé
salt and pepper
pinch of cayenne
1 teaspoon Worcestershire
    sauce
flour and water paste
biscuit dough or pastry

This good old English dish is one of the best possible uses
for leftover steak or roast. It is good enough to warrant
purchasing an extra-large steak occasionally.

Melt fat in heavy skillet and lightly brown onions. If you use lamb kidneys, quarter them and remove white tissue. If you use veal kidneys, see that the butcher doesn't strip the fat from them. Pare the fat so that a thin shell remains, split kidneys lengthwise, remove the tough white tissue, and dice kidneys. Add with steak to the skillet and brown well, stirring frequently. Add consommé and seasonings, cover, and simmer over a low flame until meat is tender, 10–20 minutes. Add more liquid if necessary, depending upon whether you use biscuit dough or pastry for top crust. Biscuit dough needs more gravy.

When the meat is very tender thicken the gravy moderately with flour and water paste, pour into casserole, cover with pastry slashed to let steam escape or small biscuits, and put in a 450° oven. After 10 minutes reduce heat to 375° and continue baking 10–15 minutes longer, or until crust is well browned.   SERVES 5–6.

SALMIS OF BEEF

4 *large slices LO roast beef*   1 *teaspoon lemon juice*
2 *tablespoons butter or*   ½ *cup dry red wine*
   margarine   1 *teaspoon Worcestershire*
2 *tablespoons flour*   *sauce*
¾ *cup consommé*

This is one of the simplest ways to make a new dish of leftover roast beef. It is even simpler if you have good gravy left over too, because you can use that instead of making a sauce.

Heat butter in large heavy skillet, blend in flour, cook a minute or two, and stir in consommé, seasoning lightly if it needs it. (If you have gravy on hand just thin it out a little and heat through.) Add lemon juice, wine, and Worcestershire sauce, stir until well blended and smooth, and lay in slices of beef. Spoon a little of the sauce over the meat, cover, and heat 2 or 3 minutes over moderate heat.   SERVES 4.

TAMALE PIE

2 cups LO roast beef
    chopped fine or
    coarsely ground
1 cup white corn meal
4 cups boiling water
2 teaspoons salt
¼ teaspoon pepper
½ tablespoon Worcester-
    shire sauce

½ cup chopped ripe olives
1 medium onion minced
1 clove garlic mashed
2 tablespoons butter or
    margarine
1½ cups canned tomatoes
1 tablespoon chili powder
½ cup fine bread crumbs

Put boiling water in top of double boiler, over direct heat, and slowly stir in cornmeal. Add half of the salt, the pepper, Worcestershire sauce, and olives. Cook over boiling water in lower pan of double boiler 15 minutes, stirring occasionally.

Heat half the butter in a skillet and lightly brown onion and garlic. Stir in meat and just heat through. Add remaining salt, tomatoes, and chili powder, and mix well. Remove from heat. Spread a thin layer of the corn meal mush on the bottom of a well-greased 2-quart casserole, then a layer of the meat-tomato mixture, and continue until ingredients are used, ending with mush. Melt remaining butter, mix with crumbs, and spread on top. Bake in 375° oven 25–30 minutes, or until well browned.   SERVES 6–8.

YORKSHIRE-BURGER SQUARES

The Yorkshire Part:
1 cup sifted flour
⅛ teaspoon salt
1 cup whole milk
2 eggs
pinch of nutmeg
dash cayenne pepper
dash of mace

The Burger Part:
3½ cups LO beef chopped
  fine
1½ tablespoons grated
  onion
1 teaspoon minced
  parsley
1 teaspoon finely cut
  chives
½ garlic clove mashed
salt and pepper
pinch of ground cloves

If you have an electric mixer make the pudding part in it. Sift flour with salt, moisten gradually with milk. Beat in whole eggs, one at a time, add seasoning, and beat 2–3 minutes. Let stand a moment while you mix well all of the ingredients in the second column. Grease well a large shallow casserole or baking pan, heat it in the oven to piping hot. Pour half of the batter in it, spread the meat mixture over it evenly but quickly, gently pour on the rest of the batter, and bake in a hot oven, 425° until pudding has risen and begins to be firm to the touch—about 20 minutes. Lower heat to 350° and continue baking another 20 minutes. Cut in squares, and serve at once with mushroom sauce.   SERVES 6.

DE LUXE CORNED-BEEF HASH

2 *cups LO corned beef*
chopped (canned will
do)
2 *cups LO boiled potatoes*
cut in small dice
1 *tablespoon bacon fat*

1 *medium onion chopped*
1 *garlic clove mashed*
1 *teaspoon Worcestershire*
sauce
3 *tablespoons dry red wine*
salt and pepper

The use of red wine here adds fine flavor to the ever-popular corned-beef hash.

Melt fat in heavy skillet and lightly brown onion and garlic in it. In a large bowl mix corned beef, potatoes, Worcestershire sauce, wine, and salt and pepper to taste, until well blended. Turn into skillet, stir well, and let cook over low heat. If you want a crusty outside do not stir, but fold over like an omelet and slide onto hot platter. If not, stir two or three times.   SERVES 6.

RED FLANNEL HASH

6 *cold boiled potatoes*
1½ *cups LO corned beef*
(or canned)
6 *medium cooked beets*
1 *large onion*

salt and pepper
dash of nutmeg
½ *cup consommé*
2 *tablespoons bacon fat*

The proper way of making red flannel hash will probably always be a matter of vigorous argument. Whether this is the best way or not, who can say? At least it is a good way.

Put potatoes, corned beef, beets, onion, and seasoning in a large wooden bowl and chop together quite fine. Moisten with consommé. Heat fat in heavy skillet, spread hash evenly, pack it down firmly, turn heat very low, and cook until bottom is brown and crusty. Fold over and slide out on hot platter. Serve with tomato sauce.   SERVES 6.

FRANKFURTERS

FRANKFURTER ROLLS

LO frankfurters   *prepared mustard*
thin slices white bread   *mayonnaise*

Leftover franks make a good and simply made hot hors d'oeuvre. For each frank you have on hand take one slice of bread, remove crusts, and spread fairly generously with mayonnaise and mustard mixed (in equal quantities). Lay the bread on a damp or wet towel, place frank at one end, and roll up quickly. Wrap in waxed paper and store in refrigerator an hour or two or even all day. At serving time cut each roll into short lengths—about 1 inch—and brown under the broiler.

FRANKFURTER SCRAMBLED EGGS

3–4 LO frankfurters cut in   *1 medium onion chopped*
½-inch lengths   *1 tablespoon paprika*
4 eggs lightly beaten with a   *1 large tomato peeled and*
fork   *cut in small wedges*
3 tablespoons butter or   *3 tablespoons sherry*
margarine   *salt and pepper*
2 tablespoons chopped
green pepper

This flavorsome dish is a good way to use up a few leftover frankfurters. If you want to make it "from scratch" use a small tin of Vienna sausages.

Melt fat in heavy skillet and lightly sauté onion and green pepper. Add paprika and frankfurters and sauté over very low heat about 5 minutes. Add tomato and sherry, with salt and pepper to taste. Cover and simmer gently about 15 minutes. Pour in eggs and stir very gently until eggs are just set.   SERVES 4.

HAM

HAM BALLS

½ cup finely ground LO
    ham
1 cup cottage cheese, quite
    dry
1 tablespoon well-drained
    prepared horseradish
½ teaspoon prepared
    mustard

¼ cup sour cream
salt and pepper
½ cup chopped watercress
    leaves or minced
    parsley
2 tablespoons finely cut
    chives

Mix well ham, cheese, horseradish, mustard, and sour cream. Add a little salt if needed and a dash of pepper. On a sheet of waxed paper spread mixed watercress and chives. Roll ham mixture into small balls, about the size of a medium olive. Roll in watercress and chives mixture until well coated. Chill, stick a toothpick in each ball, and serve with cocktails. Or make in balls the size of a small egg and serve as a luncheon or supper dish with potato salad.

HAM AND EGG COCKTAIL BALLS

4 tablespoons LO ham
    minced fine
4 hard-cooked eggs
    chopped fine
2 tablespoons flour
2 tablespoons minced
    parsley

3 tablespoons sweet cream
2 tablespoons melted butter
salt and pepper
1 raw egg
fine bread crumbs
fat for deep frying

These little ham and egg balls make a good hot hors d'oeuvre to serve with cocktails, and are very little trouble to make.

Mix thoroughly the ham, hard-cooked eggs, flour, parsley, cream, butter, and salt and pepper if necessary. Shape into small balls, a little smaller than a Ping-Pong ball. Beat the raw egg lightly with a fork, adding a tablespoon or so of water. Dip the balls first in egg and then in crumbs, and chill until ready to serve. Then fry until golden brown in deep fat heated to 385° and drain on brown paper or paper toweling. Or spread balls on a baking sheet and brown in a hot oven, 400°, 10–12 minutes. Stick a toothpick in each ball and arrange on a plate with a small bowl of hot tomato sauce (canned will do) for dunking.

HAM AND CHEESE CANAPÉS

LO ham sliced thin *garlic butter*
Cheddar cheese sliced thin *rounds of bread*

Cut ham, cheese, and bread in circles, all with the same cutter. Garlic butter is made by mashing a clove of garlic with ¼ pound of softened butter and letting it stand a while to "ripen."

Toast bread rounds on one side only. Spread untoasted side with garlic butter, lay on a round of ham and a round of cheese on top of it. Arrange on baking sheet and bake 5–7 minutes in a hot oven, 400°, or until cheese is bubbly. Serve at once.

HAM AND PATÉ SPREAD

½ cup LO cooked ham *1 small tin paté de foie gras*

This makes a nice spread for canapés or sandwiches. Grind ham with finest blade of food chopper and pound in a mortar until it is a smooth paste. Blend thoroughly with paté de foie gras and chill.

HAM SANDWICHES

1½ cups ground LO ham	½ teaspoon prepared
¼ cup chopped gherkins	mustard
	¼ cup mayonnaise

Blend ingredients well and make sandwiches with white or whole wheat bread or finger rolls.

HAM AND CHEESE TOAST

stale bread	LO ham sliced medium thin
thinly sliced cheese	butter

Slice stale bread quite thin, remove crusts, and butter fairly generously. On one slice arrange a layer of cheese, then a layer of ham, another layer of cheese, and top with a second slice of buttered bread. Press firmly together. Heat butter in heavy skillet, and when it is sizzling lay in sandwiches, using a pancake turner. Turn down heat and sauté slowly until golden brown on both sides.

HAM CASSEROLE WITH SPINACH NOODLES

2 cups LO ham chopped	½ cup sweet cream
coarsely	salt and pepper
1½ cups grated Swiss cheese	1 tablespoon butter
½ pound spinach noodles	paprika
1 cup sour cream	

Cook the noodles in plenty of boiling salted water until tender—8–9 minutes. Mix sour and sweet cream and heat to just below boiling point. Stir in half of the cheese and all of the ham. Season to taste. In a well-greased casserole put half of the noodles, half of the ham mixture, and repeat the layers. Top with remaining cheese and dot with butter.

Sprinkle with paprika and bake 25–30 minutes in moderate oven, 375°, or until lightly browned.   SERVES 4.

HAM-CHEESE-MUSHROOM SOUFFLÉ

¾ cup LO ham chopped fine
½ cup grated American cheese
¼ cup butter or margarine
3 tablespoons flour
2 cups milk
½ cup minced celery

1½ tablespoons minced pimiento
1 cup sliced sautéed mushrooms
4 eggs separated
¾ teaspoon curry powder
1½ teaspoons grated onion
salt and pepper

Melt butter in skillet, stir in flour, and add milk gradually, stirring constantly until sauce is smooth and thick. Add cheese and stir until melted. Add celery, pimiento, mushrooms, ham, well-beaten egg yolks, curry powder, and onion. Season to taste. Cool to lukewarm and fold in egg whites beaten until stiff. Turn into well-greased 6-cup casserole and bake in moderate oven, 350°, 35–40 minutes, until well browned and as firm as you want it. SERVES 5–6.

HAM-CORN SCRAMBLE

1 cup LO ham diced
1 teaspoon bacon fat
1 small onion chopped
3 eggs lightly beaten

1 medium can cream-style corn
salt and pepper

Here is one of the simplest possible ways of making leftover ham into a fine luncheon or supper dish.

Heat fat in heavy skillet, cook onion until transparent, stir in ham, and cook until ham is lightly browned. Mix eggs and corn and turn into skillet, stirring only three or four times while eggs set. Season to taste.   SERVES 4.

HAM AND CORN CUSTARD

2 cups LO ham ground
1 large can whole-kernel
    corn or 1 package
    frozen corn cooked
salt and pepper

1 tablespoon sugar
1 cup coarse bread crumbs
3 tablespoons butter
1½ cups milk
2 eggs lightly beaten

Add salt, pepper, and sugar to corn and put half of it in a 2-quart casserole. Cover with a third of the crumbs, dot with butter, and add half of the ham. Repeat the layers, and put remaining crumbs and butter on top. Mix eggs and milk and pour over casserole. Bake in moderate oven, 350°, about 30 minutes, or until firm.   SERVES 6.

HAM CUTLETS

2 cups LO ham minced
2 hard-cooked eggs
    chopped fine

1 cup undiluted cream of
    mushroom soup
salt and pepper
2 tablespoons bacon fat

Mix ham, eggs, and soup well, season to taste, and chill at least an hour, or until mixture is stiff enough to form into chop shapes. Heat fat to sizzling and brown well on both sides.   SERVES 4-5.

HAM CORNETS

6 thin slices LO baked or
    boiled ham
2 ounces paté de foie gras

3-ounce package cream
    cheese
1 tablespoon soft butter

These delicacies, made of good-sized slices of ham, make good accompaniments to a salad of mixed vegetables or to potato salad. Small ones, made of half-size slices of ham, are good served with cocktails.

Blend paté de foie gras, cream cheese, and butter until you have a smooth, soft paste. Roll ham carefully into cornucopias, fasten with toothpicks, fill with mixture, and chill until firm. Toothpicks can be removed when the filling is well chilled and firm.

HAM AND CIDER MOLD

2 *heaping cups LO ham cut*	2 *envelopes gelatin*
in julienne strips	3 *tablespoons water*
1 *quart sweet cider*	1 *tablespoon lemon juice*
1 *cup seedless raisins*	½ *teaspoon salt*
4 *whole cloves*	*dash cayenne pepper*
¼ *cup brown sugar*	*pinch nutmeg*

Here is a fine dish for a buffet meal on a hot fall day.

Soak raisins in cider 15 minutes, or until plump. Add cloves and brown sugar and heat slowly until almost boiling. Remove from fire and stir in gelatin, which has been soaked a few minutes in water, and lemon juice. When gelatin is dissolved add salt, cayenne, and nutmeg, and chill until it begins to thicken. Stir in ham and pour into a large mold rinsed in cold water. Chill until firm and unmold on chilled platter. Serve with mayonnaise to which well-drained prepared horseradish has been added to taste—any amount up to half the quantity of mayonnaise.   SERVES 8.

Note: This can also be made in a ring mold, and the center filled with mixed cooked vegetables blended with mayonnaise.

HAM AND EGGS DIVAN

8 *ham-stuffed eggs* (*see
    recipe page* 37)
1½ *cups rich cream sauce*
½–¾ *cup sharp cheese
    grated*

1 *tablespoon grated Parme-
    san cheese*
butter
paprika

This is a delicious luncheon or Sunday-night supper dish.
All it needs to make a meal is a good tossed green salad.
Hot garlic bread is likewise indicated.

Make the eggs according to the recipe on page 37, but
omit butter in the stuffing. Arrange egg halves close together in a shallow greased casserole. Make cream sauce
with 3 tablespoons butter or margarine, 2 tablespoons flour
and 1½ cups top milk. Season to taste, stir in sharp cheese,
and stir constantly until cheese is melted. Spoon sauce over
the eggs, top with grated Parmesan cheese, dabs of butter,
and paprika, and brown quickly in moderate oven, 375°,
about 20 minutes, or until golden brown.   SERVES 8.

HAM AND MACARONI CASSEROLE

1 *cup LO ham ground*
1 *cup boiled macaroni*
pinch of celery salt
½ *teaspoon prepared
    mustard*

2 *teaspoons grated onion*
1½ *cups milk*
2 *eggs lightly beaten*

A good way to use up leftover ham, making a hearty dish
out of a little meat.

Put macaroni in bottom of greased 5-cup casserole. Add
celery salt, mustard, and onion to ham, mix well, and
spread over macaroni. Mix eggs and milk and pour over.
Bake in moderate oven, 350°, about 30 minutes, or until
firm.   SERVES 4.

HAM FRITTERS

1 *heaping cup LO ham*
   ground
2 *cups sifted flour*
2 *cups boiling water*

4 *eggs*
1 *tablespoon curry powder*
   (or to taste)
cooking oil

Stir flour into rapidly boiling water and continue stirring vigorously until it leaves the sides of the pan. Lower heat and beat in eggs, one at a time, beating hard. Remove from heat and stir in curry powder and ham. Bring cooking oil to 390° and drop batter by teaspoons or tablespoons into fat, depending upon whether you want large or small fritters. Cook until golden brown all over, drain on brown paper or absorbent paper, and serve at once with either a rich cream sauce or mushroom sauce.   SERVES 5–6.

HAM IN PORT WINE AND CREAM

2 *cups thinly sliced LO*
   ham cut in 2-inch
   squares
3 *tablespoons butter or*
   margarine

½ *cup port wine*
2 *dashes Angostura bitters*
1½ *cups heavy cream*
pinch of ground cloves

This is an extremely simple, quickly prepared, and delicious way to serve some of a leftover baked ham.

Heat butter to sizzling in a heavy skillet and lightly sauté the ham. Add wine and bitters and simmer gently until half of the liquid has evaporated. Stir in cream and cloves, increase heat slightly, and stir constantly until cream is somewhat thickened. Serve on fresh buttered toast or waffles.   SERVES 4.

HAM LOAF

2 cups LO ham ground
2 tablespoons butter or
    margarine
1 small onion chopped
2 eggs well beaten
½ cup bread crumbs

2 tablespoons tomato
    catsup
2 teaspoons Worcestershire
    sauce
¼ teaspoon prepared
    mustard
salt and pepper

Brown onion lightly in hot fat and add to ham with remaining ingredients. Pile in greased loaf pan and bake 40 minutes in moderate oven, 350°, or until well browned. Turn out on hot platter and serve with one of the following sauces.   SERVES 5–6.

Raisin Sauce: Melt 2 tablespoons butter or margarine in saucepan, blend in 2 tablespoons flour, stir in 1 cup cider gradually, cook until thickened and smooth, stirring constantly, and add ¼ cup raisins.

Mustard Sauce: Blend 1 cup sour cream with 2–3 tablespoons prepared mustard and salt to taste.

Horseradish Sauce: To ½ cup whipped cream add 1 teaspoon well-drained prepared horseradish and salt to taste. Chill.

PINEAPPLE UPSIDE-DOWN HAM LOAF

ham loaf (see preceding
    recipe)
1½ tablespoons butter

2 tablespoons brown sugar
slices of pineapple (canned)
maraschino cherries

Here is an interesting and very attractive variation on plain ham loaf. Grease the sides of the pan before you start.

In the loaf pan in which you are going to bake the ham loaf melt butter and sugar together, stirring until they are well blended. Lay in pineapple slices to cover bottom and place maraschino cherry in center of each slice. Pile ham loaf on top, bake about 40 minutes in a moderate oven, 350°, and turn out on hot platter with pineapple on top.

SERVES 5–6.

HAM MOUSSE I

¾ *cup LO ham ground fine*
1 *cup consommé or chicken broth*
1 *cup tomato juice*
½ *teaspoon paprika*

1 *envelope gelatin*
¼ *cup cold water*
2 *cups cream whipped*
1 *tablespoon sherry*
salt to taste

This recipe and the following one are wonderful dishes for hot weather, and can easily be dressed up to provide the main dish at a party. This one requires less ham than the next one and is a little richer.

Mix ham, consommé, tomato juice, and paprika and bring to boil in a saucepan. Stir in gelatin which has been softened in cold water. Stir until gelatin is dissolved and chill until it begins to thicken. Fold in whipped cream, sherry, and salt to taste. Pour in mold rinsed out in cold water and chill. Unmold on chilled platter and surround with crisp watercress.

SERVES 4–5.

If you want to make this mousse into a fancy party dish, coat a chilled mold two or three times with a clear aspic, chilling it after each application and making a design with sliced truffles cut in fancy shapes, sliced hard-cooked egg, sliced pitted ripe olives or stuffed olives, thinly sliced cucumber with edges scored with a fork, or anything that pleases you. Press into aspic and chill. Fill center with mousse, chill until firm. Dip briefly in hot water before unmolding.

HAM MOUSSE II

2 cups LO ham cut in
   julienne strips
1 small onion minced
2 tablespoons butter or
   margarine
1 cup thin cream sauce
1 rounded teaspoon paprika

1 teaspoon soy sauce
1½ envelopes unflavored
   gelatin
½ cup water
1 cup heavy cream
   whipped

Cook onion lightly in melted butter. Add cream sauce
(made with 1 tablespoon butter or margarine, 1 tablespoon
flour, 1 cup milk, and seasoning to taste), paprika, ham,
and soy sauce. Soak gelatin in water and dissolve over hot
water. Stir into the ham mixture. Blend in whipped cream.
Rinse mold in cold water and pour in mixture. Chill until
firm. Unmold on chilled platter and surround with crisp watercress, deviled eggs, and wedges of ripe tomato. SERVES 6.

HAM OMELET

I. The Omelet
   6 eggs
   3 teaspoons cold water
   salt to taste
   2 tablespoons butter or
      margarine

II. The Filling
   3 tablespoons LO ham
      ground
   1 tablespoon butter or
      margarine
   1 scant teaspoon flour
   dash pepper
   dash nutmeg
   4 tablespoons light cream

Prepare the filling before you make the omelet. Melt butter in a skillet, sauté the ham lightly in it, stir in flour,
cook a moment, and blend in cream and seasonings. (Do
not salt; ham is usually salty enough.) Keep warm while
you make the omelet.

Break eggs in a bowl, add water, and beat with a fork

just enough to blend yolks and whites. Salt very lightly.
Heat large skillet or omelet pan until it is hot enough to
sizzle but not brown a tiny piece of butter. Add remaining
butter and turn pan to spread over entire bottom. Pour in
eggs, stir entire bottom lightly but quickly with the *flat* of
a fork, turn down heat, and let eggs set. When almost done,
spread ham mixture across center third. Loosen sides with
spatula, fold one side over the spread portion, then the other
over that, and slide onto a warmed platter. Serve at once.

SERVES 3–4.

HAM PIE

2 cups LO ham chopped	salt and pepper
3 tablespoons butter or margarine	¾ teaspoon nutmeg
	⅓ cup sour cream
4 tablespoons flour	½ pound cooked macaroni
1 cup milk	1 recipe plain pastry made
6 eggs well beaten	with 2½ cups flour

Make the pastry first. Roll out ⅔ of it ⅛ inch thick and
line a 2-quart casserole with it. Then melt butter in a skillet,
blend in the flour, and stir in milk, stirring constantly until
you have a smooth and very thick sauce. Remove from
heat, add eggs, salt and pepper to taste, nutmeg, sour
cream, ham, and macaroni. Pour into pastry-lined casserole.
Roll out remaining pastry, slash well to permit steam to
escape, cover casserole, and pinch edges lightly together.
Bake an hour in a slow oven, 300°. SERVES 8–10.

HAM RING

2 cups LO ham ground fine	½ teaspoon minced parsley
2 eggs separated	1 cup whipping cream
generous pinch nutmeg	2 tablespoons dry sherry
dash cayenne pepper	

Here is a delicately flavored and attractive dish to make with the scraps from a baked ham. The center of the ring can be filled with creamed mushrooms, finely chopped spinach blended with either sour or sweet cream, or buttered green peas.

Blend well-beaten egg yolks with remaining ingredients and fold in well-beaten whites gently. Turn into well-greased ring mold, set in pan of hot water, and bake about 35 minutes in moderate oven, 300°, or until top is firm to the touch. Let stand 2–3 minutes after removing from the oven and unmold on heated platter.   SERVES 6.

HAM ROLL

1½ cups LO ham chopped	1 recipe baking powder
1 scant tablespoon butter or	biscuits
margarine	1 tablespoon chopped
1 tablespoon minced onion	pimiento
1½ cups cream sauce	½ cup LO green peas
	salt and pepper

Make cream sauce first, since part of it is added to the ham. Use 2 tablespoons butter or margarine, 2 tablespoons flour, and 1½ cups top milk for the sauce. Season to taste.

Melt butter in skillet, brown onion lightly, and stir in ham. Cook only a moment. Blend in ½ cup of the cream sauce and remove from heat. Roll out or pat biscuit dough into a rectangle about ¼ inch thick. Spread with ham mixture and roll up like a jelly roll. (If you roll out the biscuit dough on a floured piece of waxed paper you can lift the paper as you roll up the dough.) With a sharp greased knife cut the roll in slices about 1 inch thick. Lay cut side up on a greased baking sheet or in a shallow oven-proof dish and bake 20 minutes in hot oven, 450°. Serve at once with cream sauce.

To make the sauce, keep cream sauce not used in the roll in a double boiler over simmering water, covered. Just before serving add pimiento and green peas.   SERVES 6.

HAM SOUFFLÉ

1 *cup cooked ham chopped fine*	½ *cup Gruyère cheese grated*
2 *cups rich cream sauce*	4 *eggs separated*
	pinch cayenne

Make the cream sauce of 3 tablespoons butter, 3 tablespoons flour, and 2 cups whole milk. If ham is very mild add a little salt. Let sauce simmer a moment and then add ham and cheese. Cook until cheese is melted. Remove from fire and add well-beaten egg yolks and cayenne. Cool to lukewarm and fold in stiffly beaten whites. Turn into well-greased 5-cup casserole and bake in moderate oven, 350°, 30–35 minutes, or until firm enough that a knife inserted in center comes out clean.   SERVES 4.

HAM AND SPAGHETTI MOLD

1 *cup LO ham chopped*	1 *egg yolk*
½ *teaspoon prepared mustard*	⅔ *cup cooked spaghetti*
	salt
1 *tablespoon wine vinegar*	⅔ *cup cream sauce*

Mix all ingredients well. Make cream sauce with 1 tablespoon butter or margarine, 1 tablespoon flour, and ⅔ cup milk. Season to taste. Pack firmly in small well-greased ring mold and bake in moderate oven, 350°, until firm, about 20–25 minutes. Unmold on heated platter, fill center with buttered green peas, and arrange sliced tomatoes around the outside.   SERVES 4.

HAM-SPINACH CASSEROLE

2 *cups LO ham diced small*
1 *pound fresh spinach or 1*
    package frozen
    chopped
1½ *cups medium cream*
    sauce

1 *cup grated sharp cheese*
2 *tablespoons buttered*
    crumbs
paprika

Cook spinach in small amount of salted water only until thoroughly wilted or thawed. Drain well, pressing with a spoon to get as dry as possible. If you use fresh spinach chop it fine. Make cream sauce with 2½ tablespoons butter or margarine, 2½ tablespoons flour, 1½ cups milk, and salt to taste. Take 1 tablespoon of the grated cheese from the cup to mix with buttered crumbs for a topping, and blend the rest of the cheese into the cream sauce. Mix ½ cup of the sauce with chopped spinach. Put half of the ham in the bottom of a medium casserole. Pour spinach over the ham and add remaining ham. Cover the whole with remaining cheese sauce and top with mixed cheese and crumbs. Sprinkle with paprika and bake about 15 minutes in a moderately hot oven, 400°, or until crumbs are brown and sauce bubbling.   SERVES 4.

HAM-STUFFED GREEN PEPPERS

2 *cups LO ham ground*
2 *large or 4 small green*
    peppers
1½ *cups LO boiled rice*
2 *tablespoons bacon or ham*
    drippings
1 *tablespoon chopped onion*

2 *tablespoons chopped*
    celery
2 *teaspoons flour*
½ *cup milk*
salt and pepper
¼ *cup grated cheese*

Prepare peppers as in recipe for Stuffed Green Peppers (p. 80). Heat fat and sauté onion and celery until yellow.

Blend in flour and milk and stir until thick and smooth. Stir in ham and rice, and season additionally if necessary. Lay pepper cases in greased shallow casserole or pie plate and fill solidly with ham mixture. Top with cheese, add 2 tablespoons of water to casserole, and bake 25–30 minutes in a hot oven, 400°.   SERVES 4.

HAM- OR TONGUE-STUFFED EGGS

¼ cup minced LO ham or tongue	1 teaspoon finely chopped gherkins or piccalilli
6 hard-cooked eggs	1 teaspoon soft butter
1 teaspoon minced parsley	mayonnaise

Slit eggs lengthwise, scoop out yolks and rub them through a fine sieve or mash well with wooden spoon. Mix yolks with meat, parsley, pickle, and butter. Blend in just enough mayonnaise to hold the mixture together. Stuff the whites with it and chill until firm.

HAM TIMBALES

2 cups LO ham chopped fine or ground	1 tablespoon minced parsley
¼ cup melted butter or margarine	¾ cup scalded milk
¾ cup soft bread crumbs	4 eggs
1 tablespoon grated onion	2 tablespoons sherry
	salt and pepper

This is not only a delicious dish, but it is also a wonderful way to make leftover odds and ends of ham go a long way.

In a good-sized saucepan mix melted butter, bread

crumbs, onion, and parsley, and cook over moderate heat until crumbs begin to brown a little. Stir in hot milk, blend well, and cook for 5 minutes over low heat, stirring constantly. Add sherry to eggs and beat well. Add eggs and ham to hot mixture and season to taste. Pour in shallow well-greased mold or 6 individual molds, filling them ¾ full. Set in pan of hot water and bake in moderate oven, 375°, 25–30 minutes, or until center is firm to the touch. Unmold on heated platter and pour rich cream sauce or mushroom sauce over and around. (Cream of mushroom soup thinned out with just a little top milk makes an acceptable mushroom sauce.)   SERVES 6.

HAM OR TONGUE AND VEGETABLE SALAD

1 *cup LO ham or tongue cut in small dice or julienne strips*
½ *cup LO cooked carrots chopped or raw carrot coarsely grated*
½ *cup LO boiled potatoes diced fine*
½ *cup LO cooked beets cut in julienne strips*
½ *cup LO string beans cut in pieces or Frenched*
½ *cup LO cooked peas*
French dressing
mayonnaise

This is a good family meal when you have leftover ham or tongue. It is quite flexible, and you can omit any one or two vegetables, increasing the amounts of the others.

Mix ingredients lightly but thoroughly and toss gently with just enough French dressing to moisten well. Chill. When ready to serve drain off any excess dressing and mix with enough mayonnaise to coat well.   SERVES 5–6.

HAWAIIAN HAM AND YAMS

2 cups LO ham coarsely
   chopped
4 medium yams or sweet
   potatoes
3 tablespoons butter or
   margarine
salt and pepper
pinch nutmeg

milk
½ cup chopped green
   pepper or pimiento
1 No. 2 can pineapple
   chunks
2 tablespoons brown sugar
1 tablespoon cornstarch
2 tablespoons vinegar

The sweet-sour flavor of the ham in this recipe, and its combination with yams or sweet potatoes makes it a real treat.

Cook potatoes in boiling salted water until tender. Peel and mash, adding 1 tablespoon butter, salt and pepper to taste, nutmeg, and enough milk to make potatoes fairly soft. (If you use yams you may not need any milk, since they tend to be juicier than sweet potatoes.)

Melt remaining 2 tablespoons butter in skillet. Lightly brown ham. Add green pepper (or pimiento) and drained pineapple chunks (reserve juice). Cook 2–3 minutes. Combine sugar and cornstarch and stir in. Combine pineapple juice and vinegar and stir in. Continue to cook until clear and thickened, stirring constantly. Pour in shallow casserole, top with large spoonfuls of potato, and bake in moderate oven, 400°, 20–25 minutes, until bubbling. SERVES 4.

ROYAL HAM WITH SWEET POTATOES

3 *cups LO ham cut in ½-*
  inch cubes
5 *medium sweet potatoes*
1 *cup mushrooms sliced*
3 *tablespoons butter or*
  margarine
3 *tablespoons flour*
2 *cups consommé*

12 *cooked Brussels sprouts*
2 *tablespoons brown sugar*
dash nutmeg
salt
½ *cup top milk*
1½ *tablespoons Angostura*
  bitters

Put potatoes on to cook in boiling salted water. Sauté mushrooms lightly in butter, blend in flour, add consommé, and stir until smooth. Put ham and sprouts in 2-quart casserole and pour mushroom sauce over. Cover and put in moderate oven, 350°. Peel potatoes, mash, add brown sugar, nutmeg, salt to taste, and milk, and whip until light and fluffy. Remove casserole from oven, stir in Angostura, and spread potatoes over the top. Increase oven heat to 425° and bake 25–30 minutes, or until brown.   SERVES 6.

SALAD RUSSE

¼ *cup LO ham chopped*
¼ *cup LO cooked carrots*
  sliced or diced small
¼ *cup LO green beans cut*
  small

¼ *cup chopped tomato*
1 *hard-cooked egg chopped*
mayonnaise thinned with
  sour cream

Mix all ingredients lightly with enough mayonnaise just to moisten well. Serve on crisp lettuce leaves or use to stuff small tomatoes.   SERVES 4–5.

SCALLOPED HAM

1 *cup chopped LO ham*
¾ *cup buttered cracker*
    crumbs

4 *hard-cooked eggs*
    chopped fine
2 *cups medium cream*
    sauce

In a small greased casserole arrange alternate layers of crumbs, eggs, cream sauce, and ham, and repeat. Save out enough crumbs to provide a top layer. Make cream sauce with 3 tablespoons butter or margarine, 3 tablespoons flour, and 2 cups milk, seasoning to taste. Bake in moderate oven, 375°, until crumbs are brown, about 15–20 minutes.

SERVES 4.

LAMB

BOBOTEE

2 *cups LO lamb chopped fine*	¼ *teaspoon pepper*
1 *slice white bread, crusts removed*	1 *teaspoon sugar*
	1 *tablespoon lemon juice or vinegar*
½ *cup milk*	
1 *tablespoon butter*	6–8 *blanched almonds chopped fine*
1 *medium onion chopped*	
2 *eggs*	¼ *cup seeded raisins or ½ cup chopped apple or 2 tablespoons chutney*
1 *tablespoon curry powder*	
½ *teaspoon salt*	
	1 *bay leaf*

This recipe comes from South Africa, where it is one of
the real classics. It is an old Cape Malay dish, and can
be made with fresh meat as well as leftover. In this case it
should be made with 2 pounds of lamb ground and the
other ingredients, except eggs and almonds, should be
doubled. Cooking time then should be 1¼ hours.

Soak the bread in the milk for a few minutes and squeeze
out as dry as possible. Reserve the milk. Melt butter and
brown onion well. Mix well the lamb, onion, soaked bread,
1 egg, curry powder, salt, pepper, sugar, lemon juice, almonds, and raisins, apple, or chutney. Beat milk and the
other egg together and stir in half, mixing all together well.
Pour in greased casserole, pour remaining egg-milk mixture
over, lay bay leaf on top, and bake in a slow oven, 300°,
40–45 minutes. Serve with rice and chutney.   SERVES 5.

LAMB CURRY

2 cups diced cooked lamb
2 medium cooking apples,
    cored, peeled, and
    sliced
1 green pepper chopped
2 medium onions sliced
1 clove garlic mashed
2 tablespoons olive or cook-
    ing oil
2 tablespoons flour
1 tablepsoon curry powder

½ teaspoon salt
pinch of marjoram
pinch of thyme
1 cup consommé
½ cup dry red wine
juice and grated rind of 1
    lemon
½ cup seedless raisins
2 whole cloves
¼ cup shredded coconut

One of the most delicious ways to transform leftover lamb into a real treat is curry, and this recipe is easier than its length suggests.

Sauté apple, green pepper, onions, and garlic in the cooking fat in a small kettle or heavy skillet. When the onions become somewhat transparent (not brown), blend in flour, curry powder, salt, and herbs. Cook 5 minutes over low heat and then stir in consommé, wine, lemon juice and rind, raisins, and cloves. Cover and simmer over lowest possible heat 20–30 minutes, stirring occasionally. Add lamb and coconut, correct seasoning and reheat.   SERVES 5–6.

Curry always improves on standing, so it is a good idea to make this in the morning and merely reheat at dinnertime. Serve with plenty of hot, fluffy rice, and any or all of the usual condiments. See recipe for Curried Chicken (p. 104).

CAPE TOWN LAMB CURRY

2 cups LO lamb diced	1 tablespoon lemon juice or
2 tablespoons butter or	vinegar
bacon fat	1 teaspoon sugar
2 medium onions chopped	salt and pepper
coarsely	1 cup consommé or chicken
2 small green apples sliced	broth
1 generous tablespoon	¼ cup milk
curry powder	flour and water paste

This is a much simpler curry than the preceding one.

Heat fat in a small heavy kettle and lightly brown onion. Add apple, curry powder, lemon juice, sugar, salt and pepper to taste, consommé, and milk. Stir well, and when it is close to boiling add the meat. Cover, lower heat, and simmer about ½ hour. Before serving thicken moderately with flour and water paste. Serve with rice and chutney.

SERVES 5–6.

LAMB AND EGGPLANT

2 cups LO lamb diced small	1 cup peeled and chopped
2 tablespoons olive oil	tomatoes (canned will
1 large onion chopped	do)
1 clove garlic mashed	1 bay leaf
1 medium eggplant peeled	½ teaspoon chervil
and cut in 1-inch cubes	½ teaspoon sweet marjoram
	salt and pepper

Served with plenty of hot fluffy rice, this dish makes good use of the tag end of a leg of lamb and at the same time provides a fine one-dish meal.

Heat olive oil in heavy skillet and lightly brown onion and garlic. Add eggplant and cook 5 minutes, stirring frequently. Add tomatoes, bay leaf, herbs, seasoning to taste, and simmer, covered, about 10 minutes, or until eggplant

is quite soft. Stir in lamb and heat until piping hot. Serve
at once.   SERVES 4–5.

LAMB, EGGPLANT, AND RICE CASSEROLE

2 cups LO lamb cut in 1-
   inch cubes
1 small eggplant cut in 1-
   inch cubes (do not
   peel)
2 tablespoons bacon fat or
   olive oil

1 medium onion chopped
salt and pepper
½ teaspoon chervil
½ teaspoon marjoram
1½ cups consommé
1 cup canned tomatoes
¾ cup raw rice

Soak the eggplant cubes in heavily salted water 15 minutes. Heat fat in heavy skillet and brown lamb cubes very
lightly. Skim out and reserve. Lightly brown onion in same
fat, and when it begins to show color stir in dry rice and
brown it lightly, stirring frequently to prevent burning.
Transfer to casserole. Lightly brown well-drained eggplant
cubes in remaining fat, adding more if necessary, and transfer to casserole. Blend in salt and pepper to taste, chervil,
and marjoram. Pour consommé in skillet to clean it out and
add to casserole with tomatoes. Cover and bake at 350°
35–40 minutes. After 20 minutes remove from oven, stir in
lamb, correct seasoning, re-cover, and finish cooking. If not
fairly dry 10 minutes before serving time, uncover to finish
cooking.   SERVES 4.

LAMB-MACARONI CUSTARD

1 cup LO lamb, chopped
   fine
1 cup LO cooked macaroni
½ teaspoon salt
⅛ teaspoon celery salt
½ teaspoon minced parsley

½ teaspoon Angostura
   bitters
½ teaspoon grated onion
1½ cups milk
2 eggs lightly beaten

This recipe gives you an entirely new dish out of two left-overs. It can be doubled or tripled to serve a big family.

Spread macaroni in bottom of a well-greased 5-cup casserole. Mix lamb well with seasonings and arrange in a layer over the macaroni. Mix eggs and milk and pour over. Bake in a 350° oven until firm, 25–30 minutes.   SERVES 4.

LAMB AND RICE CASSEROLE

2 cups LO lamb cut in ½–
   ¾-inch dice
3 tablespoons butter or
   margarine
2 medium onions minced
¾ cup dry raw rice

3 medium tomatoes peeled
   and chopped
2 cups chicken broth
salt and pepper
½ teaspoon marjoram
1 tablespoon Worcester-
   shire sauce

Leftover lamb combines with rice to make a delicious casserole just as well as uncooked lamb does. Be careful not to cook it too long, however.

Heat butter in heavy skillet, sauté onions for a moment, add dry rice, and cook until rice is yellow, stirring frequently to prevent scorching. Stir in tomatoes, cook until heated, and put mixture in 6-cup casserole. Add chicken broth, salt and pepper to taste, marjoram, and Worcestershire sauce. Cover and bake in a moderate oven, 375°, 35–40 minutes. After 15 minutes stir in the lamb, recover, and continue cooking. If rice is not quite dry at end of cooking time, remove cover, stir well, and cook an additional 5–10 minutes.   SERVES 4–5.

LAMBURGERS

2 cups LO lamb
1 small green pepper
1 medium onion
½ cup cut-up mushrooms or celery
1 egg
2 tablespoons melted butter or margarine
3 tablespoons heavy cream or sour cream

2 tablespoons fine bread crumbs
salt and pepper
1 scant teaspoon prepared mustard
2 teaspoons Worcestershire sauce
2 tablespoons bacon fat

This is a wonderful way to use the final scraps from a lamb roast.

Put lamb, pepper, onion, and mushrooms or celery through the meat grinder, using a medium blade. Add egg, butter, cream, bread crumbs, and seasonings and mix vigorously. If too soft to shape easily add more bread crumbs. If rather dry add a little more cream or a little leftover gravy. Shape into small cakes, chill well to firm them, and brown very slowly in bacon fat in heavy skillet. Serve with lamb gravy warmed up if you have any left, or tomato sauce.

SERVES 4–5.

LAMB SCALLOPINI

2 cups sliced LO roast lamb cut in pieces about 1½ inches square
2 tablespoons bacon fat or butter or margarine
2 medium onions sliced
1 small clove garlic minced
2 small green peppers sliced

1 cup LO lamb gravy thinned out with consommé or red wine
salt and pepper
2 tablespoons sherry
1 tablespoon minced parsley

Heat bacon fat to sizzling and lightly brown onions, garlic, and green peppers, stirring constantly. Blend in gravy (if you do not have leftover gravy heat 1 cup consommé and thicken slightly with flour and water paste). Season to taste, lay in lamb, stir gently, cover, and leave on low heat until very hot. Add sherry, pour in serving dish, and sprinkle with parsley.   SERVES 4.

LAMB WITH SOUR CREAM

2 *cups LO lamb cut in 1-inch cubes*
1 *tablespoon bacon fat*
1 *medium onion sliced thin*
½ *teaspoon paprika*

½ *cup tomato juice or con-sommé*
½ *cup sour cream*
1 *teaspoon minced parsley*

Heat bacon fat in heavy skillet and lightly brown onion. Add lamb pieces and sauté 2–3 minutes, long enough to brown them just a bit. Stir in paprika and tomato juice, cover, and cook over very low heat about 20 minutes. Just before serving stir in sour cream, heat well, turn out in serving dish, and sprinkle with parsley.   SERVES 4.

MOUSSAKA OF LAMB

2 *cups LO lamb diced small*
1 *eggplant cut in ½-inch dice*
2 *tablespoons bacon fat or olive oil*
1 *medium onion chopped*
1 *cup consommé or LO gravy thinned with ½ cup water*

salt and pepper
1 *tablespoon minced parsley*
2 *tomatoes cut in ½-inch slices*
½ *cup buttered bread crumbs*

Here is another lamb and eggplant combination, this time without the rice.

Cover eggplant cubes (do not peel) with boiling salted water and parboil about 5 minutes, or until barely tender. Drain. Sauté onion in bacon fat until soft but not brown and put in 6-cup casserole. Cover with alternate layers of eggplant and lamb (3 of eggplant and 2 of lamb). Pour consommé or gravy over, season to taste, sprinkle with parsley, cover, and bake in 325° oven ½ hour. Sauté tomato slices quickly in fat remaining in skillet in which onions were cooked. Remove casserole from oven, lay tomatoes on the top, cover with crumbs, and bake 10 minutes more, uncovered, or until top is browned.   SERVES 6.

SALMIS OF LAMB

8 slices LO roast lamb
2 tablespoons butter or margarine
½ tablespoon minced onion
⅓ cup sliced mushrooms
1½ tablespoons flour

1 cup consommé
½ teaspoon Worcestershire sauce
12 stuffed olives sliced
salt and pepper

Melt butter in heavy skillet and sauté onion and mushrooms until onion is yellow. Blend in flour and cook until flour is lightly browned. Stir in consommé, Worcestershire sauce, and olives. Season to taste, and lay in lamb slices. Spoon sauce over lamb, cover, and simmer over very low heat just until meat is thoroughly heated.   SERVES 4.

STUFFED LAMB ROLLS

6 *large, thin slices LO roast*   2 *tablespoons butter or*
  lamb   *margarine*
½ *cup any standard bread*   2 *tablespoons currant or*
  stuffing   *grape jelly*
½ *cup LO lamb gravy*   *salt and pepper*
  thinned out or con-
  sommé or chicken
  broth

Slice the lamb thin for this dish or you will not be able to
roll it up. Lay out slices and place a spoonful of stuffing
on each. Roll up, tie or fasten with toothpicks or skewers,
and lay in shallow greased casserole. Heat gravy in a saucepan with butter and jelly and a little salt and pepper. When
butter and jelly are dissolved pour liquid over rolls and bake
15 minutes in a hot oven, 400°, basting several times.

SERVES 6.

TURKISH EGGPLANT STUFFED WITH LAMB

3 *cups ground LO lamb*   2 *medium tomatoes peeled*
3 *small eggplants*   *and chopped*
4 *tablespoons olive oil*   2 *tablespoons chopped*
4 *tablespoons butter*   *parsley*
2 *medium onions minced*   *salt and pepper*
1 *clove garlic mashed*   2 *eggs well beaten*

Lamb, eggplant, and olive oil make a wonderful combination, and leftover lamb combines almost as well as fresh.
This recipe makes them into a very handsome mold.

Cut eggplants in half lengthwise and sauté, cut side
down, over moderate heat, in hot olive oil until well
browned. Carefully scoop out meat, beginning by cutting
around the outside about ¼ inch in, and use sharp-edged

spoon to scoop with. The skins should be about ¼ inch thick. Chop the eggplant you have dug out rather fine.

Heat butter in skillet and lightly brown onions, garlic, and chopped eggplant. Stir in lamb, tomatoes, parsley, and seasoning to taste. Cook over medium heat about 5 minutes, stirring frequently. Remove from heat and stir in eggs. Oil a quart mold and lay eggplant skins in to line it, purple side out, ends hanging over edges of mold. Fill center with lamb-eggplant mixture, fold hanging skins over it to the center, place mold in pan of hot water, and bake at 375° 45 minutes or until firm. Let stand a few minutes before unmolding. Serve with lots of tomato sauce.　　SERVES 6.

PORK

BELGIAN PORK CURRY

3 cups LO lean pork diced	3 whole cloves
1 large Spanish or Bermuda onion chopped fine	8 peppercorns bruised
	pinch of thyme
¼ cup butter or margarine	2 tablespoons curry powder
½ teaspoon celery salt	1 quart chicken or veal stock
¼ teaspoon salt	¾ cup rich cream sauce

The end of a pork roast makes a fine curry, fully as good as chicken or veal curry, though not as well known.

Melt fat in heavy skillet and cook onion until it begins to turn yellow. Add celery salt, salt, cloves, peppercorns, thyme, and curry powder and simmer about 5 minutes. Add chicken or veal stock and cook slowly about 15 minutes. Strain through a fine sieve into good-sized saucepan, bring to a boil, and gradually stir in cream sauce (made with 2 tablespoons butter or margarine, 2 tablespoons flour, and ¾ cup top milk, seasoned to taste). Bring to a boil again, stirring constantly to prevent scorching. Add pork, lower heat, and cook very slowly 15–20 minutes. This can all be done well ahead of time, even in the morning, and heated piping hot in a double boiler at dinnertime. Like all curries, this one improves on standing. Serve over plenty of hot, fluffy rice, with applesauce on the side. SERVES 8.

PORK AND RICE CASSEROLE

3 cups ground or finely
   chopped LO cooked
   pork
2 eggs beaten lightly
½ cup raw rice
1¼ cups milk

1½ teaspoons salt
¼ teaspoon pepper
½ teaspoon Worcestershire
   sauce
½ teaspoon chopped
   parsley

Mix ingredients thoroughly, turn into 6-cup greased casserole, cover, and bake 1–1¼ hours in a moderate oven, 350°. Stir two or three times during cooking. Serve with tomato sauce.   SERVES 5–6.

CHINESE PORK WITH BEAN SPROUTS

1½ cups LO pork cut in thin
   julienne strips
3 tablespoons cooking oil
½ cup chopped onion
1½ cups chicken broth
½ cup celery cut in thin
   julienne strips
½ cup sliced mushrooms

½ cup well-drained bean
   sprouts (canned)
2 tablespoons cornstarch
¼ teaspoon salt
¼ teaspoon sugar
1½ tablespoons soy sauce
2 tablespoons water

Cook onion in oil until soft but not colored. Add pork strips, chicken broth, celery, mushrooms, and bean sprouts. Cover and simmer 5 minutes. In a cup mix cornstarch, salt, sugar, soy sauce, and water to a smooth thin paste. Add to the pork mixture, stirring constantly until smooth and thickened. Correct seasoning and serve over Chinese noodles crisped in the oven or over fluffy rice.   SERVES 6.

CHINESE PORK WITH GREEN PEPPERS

1 cup LO pork chopped fine	½ cup LO green peas
2 tablespoons cooking oil	2 medium tomatoes skinned
1 clove garlic	and chopped
1 medium onion sliced thin	salt and pepper
2 shallots sliced thin	1 teaspoon sugar
2 green peppers chopped	1 teaspoon soy sauce
2 large mushrooms sliced	1 tablespoon butter
thin	2 teaspoons flour

Heat the oil and lightly brown garlic clove, onion, and shallots. Remove garlic and add green peppers. Cook 2 minutes. Add mushrooms and cook 2 minutes. Add peas and tomatoes and cook 2 minutes. Add pork and cook 2 minutes. Add salt and pepper to taste, sugar, and soy sauce. If tomatoes have made mixture rather juicy, knead flour and butter together and blend in, cooking only until thickened. If mixture is not very juicy omit flour and add just butter.   SERVES 4.

CHINESE PORK PIE

2 cups LO roast pork diced	pinch of celery leaves
2 tablespoons butter or	2 whole cloves
margarine	1 cup bean sprouts
1 clove garlic mashed	(canned)
1 leek minced (white part)	½ cup sliced water chestnuts
1½ cups LO pork gravy	(canned) or slivered
1 carrot sliced	almonds
salt and pepper	1 apple pared and chopped
½ bay leaf	1 recipe biscuits

The Chinese note in this pork pie comes from the bean sprouts and water chestnuts, which make it distinctive and good.

Melt butter in skillet and lightly brown garlic and leek.

(Use a small onion if you can't get leeks.) Add pork and brown slightly. Add gravy, thinned out considerably if it is quite thick, carrot, salt and pepper to taste, bay leaf, celery leaves, and cloves. Heat to just below the boiling point, add bean sprouts, water chestnuts, and apple, and turn into 6-cup casserole. Top with small biscuits made from your favorite recipe and rolled to ½ inch in thickness. Bake in hot oven, 450°, about 20 minutes, or until biscuits are done. The casserole can be prepared in the morning, but in that case heat it in the oven before you add the biscuit topping.   SERVES 6.

ENGLISH PORK PIE

3 *cups LO roast pork cut in*
   1-inch cubes
3 *cups sliced tart apples*
4 *tablespoons sugar*
nutmeg

ground cloves
½ *cup pork gravy thinned*
   with ¼ cup water
pastry

Make your favorite pie-crust recipe and roll out enough to line a 6-cup casserole. Fill casserole with alternate layers of pork and apples. Sprinkle each apple layer with sugar, nutmeg (just a trace), and cloves. Add gravy at the end, and cover with more rolled-out pastry, slashed several times to permit steam to escape. If you want a glazed finish, brush the top with milk or cold water. Put in a 450° oven. After 10 minutes reduce the heat to 350° and bake an additional 30 minutes, or until the apples are soft.   SERVES 6–8.

PORK AND CORN PIE

2 *cups LO pork cut in ½-inch cubes*	The Topping:
	¾ *cup sifted flour*
1 *tablespoon bacon fat or cooking oil*	2 *teaspoons baking powder*
¼ *cup chopped green pepper*	¾ *teaspoon salt*
	1 *tablespoon sugar*
¼ *cup chopped onion*	1 *egg well beaten*
2 *cups tomato sauce (canned)*	¾ *cup yellow corn meal*
	¾ *cup milk*
2 *cups whole-kernel corn (frozen or canned)*	3 *tablespoons melted butter, margarine, or cooking oil*

The cornbread topping makes this an unusual pie, and the pork and corn combination makes it hearty and good.

Brown pork cubes, green pepper, and onion in bacon fat, combine with corn and tomato sauce, and pour in 2-quart casserole. To make the cornbread topping, sift together all the dry ingredients. Combine egg, milk, and shortening, blend with dry ingredients, and stir until smooth. Pour over casserole and bake in hot oven, 400°, 30–35 minutes.

SERVES 6–8.

PORK PIE WITH POTATOES

2 *cups LO pork, coarsely ground*	1 *teaspoon minced parsley*
	pinch of ground cloves
2 *cups LO boiled potatoes diced small*	½ *cup chopped onions sautéed*
1 *cup LO cooked peas or green beans or mixture of both*	½ *cup water*
	1 *recipe pastry*

This pork pie is a marked contrast to the preceding one. Roll out your favorite pastry to ⅛-inch thickness. Use part of it to line a deep pie dish, and the balance for the top crust. Mix all of the ingredients listed here, adding a little salt if necessary. Fill the pie plate and cover with top crust, well slashed to permit steam to escape. Pinch edges together, brush top with milk or cold water, and bake 40–50 minutes in a moderately hot oven, 400°.   SERVES 6.

TONGUE

DEVILED TONGUE

3–4 *slices LO cooked*
   tongue per person
flour
egg
bread crumbs
butter or margarine

1 *teaspoon dry mustard*
pinch cayenne pepper
2 *tablespoons chopped*
   gherkins
¼ *cup tomato sauce*

Dip slices of tongue in flour, then in egg beaten lightly with a teaspoon or so of water, and then in bread crumbs. Brown lightly on both sides in butter and arrange on warm platter.

In the same skillet melt another tablespoon of butter and stir in remaining ingredients. When well blended and hot, spoon over browned slices of tongue. This amount of sauce will serve for a dozen slices.

TONGUE CASSEROLE

12 *thin slices LO tongue*
2 *sour gherkins*
3 *scallions (green onions)*
   or 2 slices white onion
1 *teaspoon parsley*

¼ *cup bread crumbs*
¼ *cup dry white wine*
½ *teaspoon salt*
pepper
3 *tablespoons butter*

This is a delectable way to dress up leftover tongue.

Chop pickles, scallions, and parsley together very fine. Mix with crumbs, wine, and salt and pepper to taste. Melt half of the butter in the bottom of a shallow casserole and spread over it half of this mixture. Arrange slices of tongue over, and top with the other half of the mixture. Dot with remaining butter and bake 20 minutes at 350°. Serves 4. If you want to serve a larger number, increase the mixture proportionally and overlap slices of tongue, using as many slices as you want.

TONGUE HASH

2 cups LO tongue diced
  small or coarsely
  chopped
2 cups potatoes diced small
½ cup minced onion

2 teaspoons minced parsley
chicken or tongue broth
½ teaspoon sweet marjoram
salt and pepper

This recipe makes good use of the very end of a baked tongue, utilizing all the scraps.

Lightly mix tongue, potatoes, onion, and parsley in a large skillet. Pour over just enough chicken broth, or broth in which tongue was boiled, to moisten. Simmer over low to moderate heat. As it begins to bubble sprinkle with marjoram and add a little salt and pepper if necessary. Cover and cook over low heat about 20 minutes to ½ hour, or until potatoes are tender. Stir two or three times, and if it gets quite dry add a bit more liquid.   SERVES 4–5.

TONGUE AND POTATO SALAD

1 cup LO cooked tongue
  cut in julienne strips
3 medium LO cooked
  potatoes cut in small
  dice
¼ cup thin slices scallions
  (young green onions)
  or 3 shallots sliced thin

¼ cup chopped sweet pickle
¼ cup sour cream
½ cup mayonnaise
1 tablespoon vinegar

This is a good use for leftover tongue. Like all potato salads, however, it is better if the potatoes are freshly cooked, though leftover ones will do.

Lightly mix tongue, potatoes, scallions, and pickle. Mix

separately sour cream, mayonnaise, and vinegar, and blend gently with tongue-potato mixture. If potatoes were not well salted you may need a little salt.   SERVES 4.

PIQUANT TONGUE ROLLS

6 *large or* 12 *small slices LO tongue, rather thin*	1 *generous teaspoon capers or chopped gherkins*
½ *teaspoon chervil*	6 *anchovies mashed*
1 *teaspoon minced parsley*	4 *slices crisply cooked bacon crumbled*
2 *tablespoons shallots or onions minced*	1 *scant tablespoon butter or margarine*
½ *teaspoon tarragon*	

This is a true gourmet dish, a wonderful choice if you have enough tongue left over to cut good slices. Preferably cut them on a slant to make them larger.

Mix all the ingredients except tongue, mashing them to a paste with butter. Lay out the tongue slices and spread the mixture smoothly over them. Cut cooking parchment into squares of about 6 inches and grease the surface lightly to prevent sticking. Roll up each slice of tongue, firmly but not too tightly, and lay each one on a greased square. Wrap securely, folding in ends before you finish rolling the little packages. Lay close together, seam side down, in a small casserole or pie plate, and bake 15 minutes in a hot oven, 450°. Unwrap on heated serving plate. (Aluminum foil can be used to wrap the rolls instead of cooking parchment.)   SERVES 3.

ZIPPY TONGUE MOLD

2 cups LO tongue ground
    or chopped fine
1 tablespoon gelatin
1 cup consommé or chicken
    broth
¼ cup drained prepared
    horseradish

½ cup mayonnaise
¼ cup minced green pepper
1 tablespoon minced onion
½ teaspoon dry mustard

Soak gelatin in ¼ cup of the broth or consommé. Heat rest
of liquid and dissolve gelatin in it. Cool to lukewarm and
stir in all remaining ingredients. Turn into mold rinsed in
cold water and chill until set.   SERVES 5–6.

TONGUE- OR LAMB-STUFFED EGGPLANT

1½ cups LO tongue or lamb
    coarsely ground or
    chopped
1 large eggplant
2 tablespoons olive oil or
    bacon fat
½ cup chopped celery

1 tablespoon minced
    parsley
¼ cup minced onion
1 cup lightly buttered
    crumbs
½ teaspoon chervil
½ teaspoon marjoram
salt and pepper

Cut the stem from the eggplant with great care, so as not
to cut more than necessary of the vegetable itself. Cut in
half lengthwise and parboil 15 minutes in boiling salted
water. Turn the halves two or three times to cook evenly.
Drain well and dig out as much of the pulp as possible,
leaving at least ⅜ inches all around. Start by cutting a line
around inside the edge with a sharp knife, and dig the
pulp out with a sharp-edged spoon. Chop the removed pulp
coarsely. Melt fat in skillet and lightly sauté celery, parsley,
and onion. Add chopped eggplant and sauté 3 or 4 minutes
more. Remove from fire and stir in half of the bread crumbs,

the chervil, marjoram, tongue, and salt and pepper to taste. If the mixture seems quite dry add a bit of milk to moisten it. If it is quite moist add another tablespoon or two of bread crumbs. Heap into eggplant shells carefully, so as not to break the shells. Top with remaining ½ cup of crumbs. Arrange in greased flat casserole, add about a tablespoon of water in the bottom, and bake in a moderate oven, 350°, half an hour, or until top is well browned. To serve, cut with a sharp knife right across the shell, and serve shell and stuffing together. Serves 6–8, depending on size of eggplant.

VEAL

BLANQUETTE OF VEAL

3 cups LO veal cut in ¾-
    inch cubes
½ cup butter or margarine
3 tablespoons flour
2 cups chicken broth or
    consommé
salt and pepper
1 small bay leaf

½ garlic clove mashed
2 shallots or ½ small onion
    minced
2 tablespoons minced
    parsley
6 small white onions
¼ pound sliced mushrooms
2 tablespoons sherry

This is one of the best ways to use leftover roast veal, and
it is even better if you substitute ½ cup of dry white wine
for that much of the liquid called for.

Melt butter in heavy skillet, blend in flour, and cook
briefly but don't let it brown. Stir in liquid gradually, stirring constantly until sauce is smooth and thickened. Season
to taste and add bay leaf, garlic, shallots or onion, parsley,
and veal. Cover and simmer over lowest possible heat 5
minutes. Add onions and simmer 10 minutes longer. Add
mushrooms and cook another 10 minutes. Remove bay leaf,
add sherry, and serve with plenty of fluffy rice or buttered
noodles.   SERVES 6.

JELLIED VEAL LOAF WITH NUTS

1½ cups LO veal chopped   2 tablespoons minced
   fine   parsley
2 cups hot veal stock or   2 teaspoons minced onion
   chicken broth   ½–¾ cup chopped Brazil
1 package lemon Jello   nuts
1 teaspoon vinegar   2 eggs beaten slightly

This is a delicately flavored and delicious dish for hot
weather.

Dissolve Jello in the hot stock, and pour ⅓ of it in the
bottom of a loaf pan or ring mold rinsed out with cold water. Chill until almost set. Mix remaining ingredients with
the rest of the gelatin mixture. When the mold is ready
fill with mixture and chill until firm. Unmold on chilled
platter and serve with mayonnaise.   SERVES 6.

FLEMISH VEAL

2 cups LO veal cut in 1-   2 tablespoons crisply
   inch cubes   cooked bacon
2 tablespoons bacon fat,   crumbled
   butter, or margarine   ½ cup condensed tomato
1 large onion sliced   soup
1 clove garlic   ½ cup sautéed sliced mush-
½ teaspoon curry powder   rooms
   (opt.)   2 tablespoons sherry or ¼
½ cup boiling water   cup beer
                                  ½ cup sour cream

Lots of flavors combine here to counteract the blandness
of veal, and a delicious effect they produce!

Melt fat in heavy skillet and sauté lightly the onion and
the garlic clove stuck on a toothpick to be retrieved before
serving. As soon as the onions show a little color add veal
and continue cooking until veal is delicately browned. Stir

in curry powder, boiling water, bacon, and tomato soup. Cover and simmer over very low heat about 20 minutes. Five minutes before serving add mushrooms and sherry or beer. Just before serving stir in sour cream and allow it to heat. Serve over buttered noodles, and for a pleasant touch add a generous teaspoon of poppy seeds to the noodles just before serving. SERVES 5–6.

VEAL AND HAM PIE

2 slices LO veal ½ inch
    thick, cut in ¼-inch
    cubes
2 slices boiled ham or LO
    baked ham ½ inch
    thick, cut in ¼-inch
    cubes
2 shallots or 2 tablespoons
    onion

½ cup mushrooms, canned
    or fresh
2 tablespoons parsley
4 tablespoons bacon fat
2 large or 3 small eggs
salt and pepper
pastry

This is a very flavorful pie of the solid type (without juice) that is good either hot or cold.

Trim the meat carefully before you cut it up and put the trimmings through the meat grinder, using the finest blade, along with the shallots or onion, mushrooms, and parsley. Mix this well with bacon fat. Beat in eggs, one at a time, and season to taste. Line 6-cup casserole with pastry rolled out to ⅛ inch in thickness. Fill with alternate layers of cubed meat and egg mixture. Cover with pastry gashed several times to permit steam to escape. Bake in a slow oven, 300°, 1½ hours, or until crust is golden. SERVES 4–6.

FRICASSEE OF VEAL

2–3 cups LO boiled,
    braised, or roast veal
    cut in good-sized dice
2 tablespoons butter,
    margarine, or bacon fat
3 tablespoons coarsely
    chopped onions
1 clove garlic crushed
1 cup dry white wine
1 cup chicken broth or LO
    gravy thinned
½ small bay leaf

½ teaspoon thyme
salt and pepper
12 tiny white onions lightly
    browned in butter
12–15 tiny whole mush-
    rooms, or ¼ pound
    sliced, sautéed lightly
1 teaspoon chopped parsley
3 tablespoons butter or
    margarine kneaded
    with 2 tablespoons
    flour

Heat fat in bottom of small kettle and brown chopped onions in it lightly. Add garlic, wine and broth or gravy, bay
leaf, thyme, and salt and pepper, cover, and simmer 5 minutes. Add the little white onions and continue to simmer
until they are tender—5–10 minutes if they are quite small.
Add mushrooms and veal, bring to a boil, correct seasoning, stir in parsley, and thicken with butter and flour
kneaded together. Serve over fluffy rice, buttered noodles,
or hot cornbread split and buttered.   SERVES 6–8.

VEAL AND NOODLE CASSEROLE

2–3 cups LO veal cut in ½-
    inch cubes
8-ounce package medium
    noodles
2 tablespoons butter or
    margarine
1 medium onion chopped
1 cup coarsely chopped
    celery

salt and pepper
1 teaspoon paprika
¾ cup sliced mushrooms
    sautéed
¾ cup sour cream
2 tablespoons buttered
    bread crumbs

Cook noodles in boiling salted water until just tender, about
7 minutes. Drain. While they are cooking melt butter in

heavy skillet and lightly brown onion and celery. Add veal and continue cooking until veal is lightly browned, stirring frequently. Season with salt and pepper and stir in paprika. Add mushrooms, noodles, and sour cream, turn into greased 2-quart casserole, top with crumbs, and bake 25–30 minutes in moderate oven, 375°.   SERVES 5–6.

VEAL STROGANOFF

2 cups LO roast veal sliced
    thin and cut in strips
    about 1 x 3 inches
2 tablespoons lemon juice
4 tablespoons butter or
    margarine

1 medium onion sliced thin
1 cup mushrooms sliced
salt and pepper
1 cup sour cream

This dish is almost as delicious as the more famous Beef Stroganoff, but it can be made successfully only if the veal has not been cooked to the point where it falls to pieces. The pieces of veal used here must stay whole.

Before you start cooking, lay out the veal and dribble the lemon juice over it. Melt half the butter in a heavy skillet and cook onions and mushrooms lightly, just until onions begin to show a trace of color. In another skillet heat balance of butter to sizzling, turn in veal, and quickly sauté to golden brown. Season both veal and onion-mushroom mixture to taste. Combine mixtures and stir in sour cream. Continue cooking until well heated, stirring constantly. (If you want the sauce slightly thickened, stir 1 tablespoon flour into the cooked onion-mushroom mixture and let cook a moment.) Serve at once on plenty of hot fluffy rice.   SERVES 6.

VEAL PIE

2 cups LO cooked veal
  chopped fine
½ cup fresh bread crumbs
¼ cup milk
2 tablespoons minced onion
  sautéed lightly
1 tablespoon minced
  parsley

salt and pepper
¼ cup chopped mushrooms
  sautéed lightly (opt.)
1 egg beaten slightly
4 tablespoons LO veal
  gravy or cream
pastry

Cover crumbs with milk, let stand a few minutes, and press out milk not absorbed. Mix crumbs, veal, onion, parsley, salt and pepper to taste, mushrooms, egg, and gravy or cream to moisten well. Line a shallow casserole or deep pie plate with pastry rolled out ⅛ inch thick. Pour in veal mixture, cover with pastry top rolled thin and slashed to let steam escape, and brush top with cream, milk, or cold water. Bake in moderate oven, 375°, 35–40 minutes, or until crust is golden brown.   SERVES 4.

VEAL PIE WITH SOUR CREAM

2–3 cups LO roast veal cut
  in ¾-inch cubes
flour
2 tablespoons bacon fat
salt and pepper
¾ cup boiling chicken broth
  or water
12 small white onions

1 cup carrots diced small
1 cup sliced mushrooms
2 teaspoons minced parsley
½ teaspoon celery salt
¼ teaspoon nutmeg
1 cup sour cream
pastry or biscuit dough

The blandness of veal always needs something to "pick it up," and that something is provided here by the combination of nutmeg, mushrooms, and sour cream.

Shake up the pieces of veal lightly in a little flour in a paper bag. Heat fat to sizzling in heavy skillet and brown the meat lightly and quickly on all sides. Season (lightly if the original roast was well seasoned) and reserve. Pour broth in skillet to scrape out all the brown glaze. Stir in onions, carrots, mushrooms, parsley, celery salt, and nutmeg. Put in 6-cup casserole, cover, and bake in moderate oven, 375°, 15 minutes. Stir in browned veal and cook 15 minutes more. Remove from oven, stir in sour cream, and top with pastry slashed to let steam escape or with small baking-powder biscuits rolled or patted ½ inch thick. Increase oven heat to 450° and bake 20 minutes. SERVES 5–6.

Note: You can make this recipe as a sort of ragout, without pie topping, and serve on buttered noodles or fluffy rice. In that event cook 5 minutes after the sour cream is added.

VEAL TETRAZZINI

2 cups LO veal chopped
    medium fine
8-ounce package medium
    noodles
2 tablespoons butter or
    margarine
1 tablespoon chopped onion
2 tablespoons flour
1 cup cream

1 cup chicken broth
1 cup sliced mushrooms
    sautéed (opt.)
1 tablespoon white wine
    (opt.)
1 tablespoon sherry (opt.)
salt and pepper
¼ cup grated Parmesan
    cheese

This is one of the better ways of dressing up leftover veal.

Cook noodles in a large amount of boiling salted water until tender, about 7 minutes. Drain. While noodles are cooking, melt fat in skillet, add onion and cook a moment, add veal and cook 2 or 3 minutes, stir in flour, and gradually add cream and chicken broth mixed. Add mushrooms and wines if you are using them (you lose a good part of the flavor if you omit them), season to taste, simmer about 5 minutes. Spread noodles on the bottom of a large, shallow, well-greased casserole, pour the veal mixture carefully on top, top with cheese, and bake in a hot oven, 425°, 10–15 minutes, until cheese is well browned. SERVES 6.

VIENNA VEAL SOUFFLÉ

2 cups LO lean veal
   chopped fine
¾ tablespoon butter or
   margarine
¾ tablespoon paprika
1 tablespoon minced chives
1 teaspoon minced shallots
   or onion
½ cup chopped mushrooms
   sautéed lightly

salt
dash of cayenne pepper
½ teaspoon marjoram
½ cup heavy cream
3 egg whites beaten stiff
1 tablespoon chopped
   blanched almonds

Knead butter and paprika together and add to mushrooms
with chives and shallots. Stir in chopped veal and season
with salt to taste, cayenne pepper, and marjoram. Add
cream, mix well, and fold in egg whites. Pour gently in
medium greased casserole, sprinkle top with almonds, set
in pan of hot water, and bake 15–20 minutes at 425°.

VIENNA VEAL CASSEROLE

2–3 cups LO veal cut in ¾-
   inch cubes
2 tablespoons butter or
   margarine
1 large onion sliced
1 scant tablespoon flour
1 cup water
1 small bay leaf

2 whole cloves
½ teaspoon whole allspice
1 teaspoon caraway seeds
salt and pepper
1 scant teaspoon paprika
1 teaspoon lemon juice
¾ cup sour cream

In this flavorsome veal casserole the added flavor is provided by the boiled spices.

Melt fat in heavy skillet and sauté onions until they begin to look transparent. Add veal cubes and sauté over
medium heat just until they are delicately browned all
over, stirring frequently. While this is cooking boil the wa-

ter, bay leaf, cloves, allspice, and caraway seeds briskly for 8–10 minutes. Sprinkle paprika and flour over meat-onion mixture and stir until absorbed. Strain cooked spices and add liquid to skillet. Stir until smooth and thickened, cover, and simmer over very low heat about 15 minutes. Correct seasoning, and stir in lemon juice and sour cream. Allow just to heat through. Serve over fluffy rice or buttered noodles. SERVES 5–6.

MIXED MEATS

CHEF'S SALAD

2 cups LO chicken	1 cup celery
1 cup LO cooked tongue	2 cups heart of lettuce
1 cup cooked ham	½ cup French dressing
½ cup Swiss cheese	garnishes (see below)

This delectable salad is a standard dish of most good restaurants, and makes a wonderful luncheon or Sunday-night supper dish. It can, of course, be made with boiled ham and canned chicken and tongue, all of which are readily obtainable in most markets.

Cut all ingredients in julienne strips about 2 inches long. Toss lightly but thoroughly with French dressing. Line a large bowl with crisp lettuce leaves and turn in the salad. Garnish with wedges of hard-cooked eggs, wedges of ripe tomatoes, watercress, radish roses, and big black olives, or any combination of these.   SERVES 6–8.

MEAT AND POTATO PIE

1 cup any LO meat or chicken, minced	1 cup rich cream sauce
2 cups LO (or fresh) mashed potatoes	4 hard-cooked eggs chopped coarsely
1 tablespoon melted butter or margarine	1 teaspoon minced parsley
2 eggs well beaten	½ cup cream whipped
1 tablespoon bacon cut fine	salt
	1 tablespoon butter
	paprika

Beat potatoes vigorously with butter and beaten eggs. Stir in meat, bacon, cream sauce (made with 2 tablespoons butter or margarine, 2 tablespoons flour, and 1 cup whole milk), chopped eggs, parsley, and cream. Pour in small casserole, dot with butter, sprinkle with paprika, and bake in moderate oven, 375°, 30–35 minutes, or until somewhat puffed and delicately browned. SERVES 4.

CREAMED MEAT PIE

(LO ham, veal, chicken, or canned tuna or salmon)

2 cups meat cut in ¾-inch
    cubes or fish broken in
    chunks
2 tablespoons butter or
    margarine
1 cup thinly sliced celery
1 medium onion sliced thin
¼ cup sliced mushrooms,
    fresh or canned

½ teaspoon minced parsley
¾ cup LO cooked peas
    (opt.)
3 cups cream sauce
biscuit dough
1 cup grated Cheddar
    cheese

This is an easy way to make a little leftover meat go a long way, and is also good with a mixture of meats: ham and veal, ham and chicken, chicken and tuna, or tuna and salmon. The pie can be made in the morning and have the biscuit top added at dinnertime. In this case let the casserole heat through before adding the biscuits.

Melt fat in skillet and cook celery, onion, and mushrooms lightly, but do not brown. Add meat or fish and cook just enough to heat through. Make cream sauce with 4 tablespoons butter or margarine, 4 tablespoons flour, and 3 cups rich milk. Salt to taste, blend well with mixture in skillet, and stir in parsley and peas. Turn into 2-quart casserole. Make biscuits from your favorite recipe, add cheese before stirring in milk, roll or pat to ½-inch thickness, cut with small biscuit cutter, and arrange on top of casserole to make a closely fitting topping. Bake in 425° oven 15 minutes or until top is well browned. It will take a few minutes longer if the creamed mixture is cool. SERVES 5.

HASH SOUFFLÉ

1 *cup LO meat ground—beef, veal, lamb, or ham*	¼ *cup grated sharp cheese*
	1 *tablespoon grated onion*
½ *cup soft bread crumbs*	2 *tablespoons catsup or chili sauce*
milk	
1 *cup thick white sauce*	2 *eggs separated*
	salt and pepper

Leftover scraps from a roast are here made into a delicious dish, which can be baked either in a soufflé dish or in a ring mold, to be unmolded on a hot platter and the center filled with creamed mushrooms or creamed mixed vegetables. This same recipe can also be used to stuff green peppers or scooped-out summer squash which have been parboiled a few minutes.

Soak bread crumbs in as much milk as they will absorb and let stand a few minutes. Squeeze dry and mix with meat, cream sauce (made with 3 tablespoons butter or margarine, 3 tablespoons flour, 1 cup milk, and seasoning to taste), cheese, onion, and catsup. Stir in well-beaten egg yolks, season to taste, and fold in stiffly beaten egg whites. Put in well-greased soufflé dish or casserole, set in pan of hot water, and bake 30–40 minutes in moderate oven, 325°, or until firm to the touch in center.   SERVES 4.

MEAT AND VEGETABLE SALAD

1½ cups LO meat cut in
    julienne strips (beef,
    lamb, ham, chicken, or
    mixture)
2 cups shredded crisp
    lettuce
1 bunch crisp watercress
    with stems removed
½ cup sliced cooked beets
    (LO) cut in julienne
    strips

¼ cup sliced radishes
    (unpeeled)
½ cup chopped celery
¼ cup sliced cucumber cut
    in julienne strips
1 large tomato peeled and
    cut in thin wedges
¼ cup thin onion slices
1 teaspoon grated onion
French dressing

Arrange in a large bowl everything but grated onion and French dressing. Add onion to dressing and toss whole salad lightly but well. Serve immediately.   SERVES 6.

MACARONI WITH MEAT

2 cups ground LO beef or
    lamb
1 pound macaroni
4 tablespoons butter or
    margarine
2 medium onions chopped

1 medium tomato peeled
    and chopped
salt and pepper
¾ cup grated sharp cheese
1 cup thin cream sauce
1 egg well beaten

With a tossed green salad or a mixed vegetable salad this casserole makes a hearty one-dish meal.

Cook macaroni in a large amount of well-salted water until it is as tender as you want it, probably 10–12 minutes. (If you use the long straight variety break it up before cooking.) Drain, run cold water over it, and drain again.

Melt butter in heavy skillet and cook onions until they begin to color. Add meat and cook a minute or two, then add tomato, salt and pepper to taste, and ½ cup of the cheese. Stir until well blended. Put half the cooked macaroni in a large well-greased casserole, cover with the meat mixture, and add the remaining macaroni. Stir the egg into the cream sauce (made with 1½ tablespoons butter or margarine, 1½ tablespoons flour, 1 cup milk, and salt to taste), mix with remaining ¼ cup grated cheese, and pour over top of casserole. Bake in moderate oven, 350°, 35–40 minutes, or until well browned.   SERVES 5–6.

SAVORY SCRAMBLED EGGS

½ cup chopped LO ham,
   liver, sausage, or dried
   beef
4 eggs
4 tablespoons milk or thin
   cream

½ teaspoon chopped parsley
salt
2 tablespoons butter, margarine, or bacon fat

A little leftover meat and a few eggs can make a very flavorful luncheon or supper dish.

Break eggs into a bowl, add milk and parsley, and salt only if meat is not very salty. Beat with a fork, just enough to blend well. Heat fat to sizzling in heavy skillet, turn in eggs, reduce heat immediately, stir eggs gently, and as soon as they begin to set add meat. Continue to stir gently until eggs are as firm as you like them.   SERVES 3–4.

MEAT SHORTCAKE

2 cups LO beef, lamb, or
   pork cut in ½-inch dice
2 tablespoons bacon fat
2 tablespoons minced onion
1 clove garlic mashed
2 tablespoons flour
1 cup dry red wine
½ cup consommé or chicken
   broth

½ cup chopped mushrooms
   lightly sautéed
1 cup LO cooked peas
¼ teaspoon thyme
pinch of mace
1 tablespoon Worcestershire
   sauce
salt and pepper
biscuit dough

Heat fat in skillet and sauté onion and garlic until faintly colored. Blend in flour, cook a moment, and stir in wine and consommé or broth. When it is smooth and somewhat thick add remaining ingredients and season to taste. Keep hot in double boiler.

Make up your favorite biscuit recipe (or use Bisquick) and roll or pat it out in two rectangles ½ inch thick. Bake 12 minutes in hot oven, 425°. Place one on heated platter, pour meat mixture over, and lay the second on top. Serve at once.   SERVES 6.

RISOTTO MILANESE

¾ cup chopped LO meat
   (beef, lamb, veal, pork,
   or ham, or mixture of
   these)
4 tablespoons butter or margarine or cooking oil
½ medium onion minced

1 cup raw rice
2 cups consommé or
   chicken broth
salt and pepper
½ teaspoon saffron (opt.)
½ cup grated Parmesan
   cheese

This is a very useful dish, because it utilizes almost anything you have in the way of leftover meats, and can also be made with leftover flaked fish. Leftover cold cuts can also be used in it.

Heat butter in heavy skillet, preferably cast iron, add onion and rice, and stir almost constantly until rice is lightly browned and onion is soft. Add liquid and meat or fish leftovers, stir well, cover tightly, and simmer over lowest possible heat about 20 minutes, or until rice is tender. Stir once more, season to taste, add saffron and cheese, and continue to cook until cheese is melted.   SERVES 4.

Note: The time indicated is for converted rice. Ordinary rice will take somewhat longer and brown rice will take at least twice as long.

SHEPHERD'S PIE

2 cups LO meat diced small or ground (beef, lamb, or veal)
3 tablespoons bacon fat
2 medium onions chopped
1 small green pepper chopped
2 tablespoons celery chopped
3 tablespoons flour
2 cups milk, consommé, or leftover gravy thinned with water
salt and pepper
1 tablespoon Worcestershire sauce
1 cup cooked sliced carrots
1 cup whole-kernel corn
2 cups hot mashed potatoes
1 tablespoon butter
paprika

Shepherd's pie can be made in a great variety of ways: It can be made with practically no liquid, so that the meat part is rather solid. The carrots and corn can be omitted. The potato can be used in two layers, one on the bottom and one on the top, or it can be arranged in a ring on top of the meat instead of covering it. See page 153 for a Shepherd's Pie made with leftover seafood.

Heat fat in heavy skillet and sauté lightly onions, green pepper, and celery. If you use milk or consommé for liquid, stir in flour, cook a moment, and add liquid gradually. If you have leftover gravy, thin it out and add without using flour. Season to taste, add Worcestershire sauce, meat, and vegetables. Pour in 2-quart casserole, spread well-whipped potatoes on top, dot with butter, sprinkle with paprika, and bake in moderate oven, 350°, 20 minutes or until top is brown.   SERVES 6.

STUFFED ACORN SQUASH

1½ cups LO chicken or meat
    chopped fine
2 medium acorn squash
salt and pepper

¾ cup cream sauce
1 teaspoon minced parsley
1 cup buttered bread
    crumbs

Practically any leftover meat can be used in this way, but roast pork or ham are best.

Cut squash crosswise and scoop out seeds and membranes. (If ends are pointed slice off enough to permit squash to stand level.) Salt and pepper insides, turn upside down on lightly greased baking sheet, and bake in 375° oven about 35–45 minutes, depending on size of squash. After 15 minutes turn squash right side up and continue baking until you can prick fleshy part easily with a fork. Remove from oven.

Make cream sauce with 1½ tablespoons butter or margarine, 1½ tablespoons flour, and ¾ cup milk, seasoning to taste. Mix meat with cream sauce and parsley and fill cavities of squash, extending filling clear to edges. Cover with thick layer of crumbs and continue cooking until crumbs are brown—about 15 minutes.   SERVES 4.

STUFFED GREEN PEPPERS

1½ cups chopped LO beef,
    lamb, or veal
2 large green peppers or 4
    small ones
2 tablespoons bacon fat
2 tablespoons chopped
    celery

2 tablespoons chopped
    onion
¾ cup cooked tomato with
    juice or juice alone
1 cup bread crumbs
salt and pepper
1 tablespoon butter or
    margarine

Split peppers lengthwise, remove seeds and membrane, and parboil 2–3 minutes in boiling salted water. Drain and turn carefully upside down to drain further.

Heat bacon fat in skillet and sauté celery and onion until yellow. Add meat, tomato or juice, bread crumbs, and salt and pepper to taste. Lay pepper halves right side up in greased shallow casserole or pie plate and fill solidly with mixture. Sprinkle tops with additional bread crumbs, dot with butter, add about 2 tablespoons water to casserole, and bake 25–30 minutes in a hot oven, 400°.   SERVES 4.

STUFFED TOMATO LUNCHEON

LO meat cut small or
    julienned
LO cooked vegetables
cheese cut in small dice
finely chopped onion

grated carrot
thinly sliced celery
minced parsley
mayonnaise
tomatoes

No quantities are given here, because it will depend entirely upon what you have on hand and the number of people you want to serve with it. Start with whatever meat you have on hand, supplementing leftover cooked meat with a little baloney, salami, boiled ham, or other cold cuts, or even a can of chicken if you need more meat than you have available. Add about half as much cubed cheese as you have meat. Add almost any leftover vegetables except creamed ones, in any amounts from a teaspoon to ½ cup or more. Provide a little crispness by fresh carrot and/or celery, if you are not using cooked ones. Even a little cucumber diced small can be added, or a chopped hard-cooked egg or two. Stir in enough mayonnaise to moisten well. (Flavor will be added if you mix a little curry powder or sour cream with the mayonnaise.)

Pour boiling water over the tomatoes—one good-sized one or two small ones per serving. Let stand about 2 minutes, drain, and skin. Holding each one carefully, cut off the top and scoop out the insides with a sharp-sided spoon. Chop up the scooped-out tomato and add to the filling. Add a little salt and pepper if needed. Lightly salt the insides of the tomatoes and turn them upside down to drain a few minutes. Then lay them on crisp lettuce, fill to overflowing with mixture, sprinkle with minced parsley, and serve with toasted cheese sandwiches for a delicious and hearty luncheon.

POULTRY

POULTRY

CHICKEN

CHICKEN-ALMOND SANDWICHES

2 cups LO chicken ground
½ cup blanched almonds
  ground

2 tablespoons grated pineapple well drained
3 tablespoons mayonnaise
buttered bread

These sandwiches are delicious for a special occasion—a tea party, or with fruit salad for a company luncheon or Sunday supper. Blend ingredients well, spread quite generously on thin slices of white bread, and add top slices. Remove crusts. Makes 12–15 whole sandwiches (uncut), depending upon size of slices.

COLD CHICKEN SOUP

1 cup LO chicken chopped
  fine
3½ cups chicken broth
½ teaspoon curry powder

4 egg yolks well beaten
2 cups light cream
salt

This is a delicious soup for a summer luncheon. If you use canned chicken broth, boil it down to condense it somewhat.

Put chicken broth, chicken, and curry powder in soup kettle and bring slowly to a boil. Add a little of the hot stock to the egg yolks, blend with cream, and slowly stir into the hot soup, stirring constantly over low heat until slightly thickened. Adjust seasoning and chill. Serve with chopped chives sprinkled on each plate. Serves 6–8 depending upon whether served in cups or plates.

CHICKEN SOUP

carcass of chicken
1 small onion sliced
2 sprigs parsley
¼ cup celery leaves
salt and pepper

5 cups water
4 teaspoons pearl barley or rice
¼ cup finely chopped carrot
½ cup thinly sliced celery
minced parsley

Break up the chicken carcass, smashing larger bones with cleaver or hammer. Put in large soup kettle with onion, sprigs of parsley, and celery leaves, add a teaspoon or so of salt and the water, cover, and simmer about 2 hours. Strain and salvage all bits of meat that have separated from bones. Add to broth with pearl barley or rice, carrot, celery, and salt and pepper to taste. Simmer gently until barley or rice is tender, 20–30 minutes. Sprinkle minced parsley over each serving. Serves 6–8, depending upon whether it is served in cups or soup plates.

CHICKEN SALAD ROLLS

2 cups chopped LO chicken
2 cups celery chopped coarsely
1 green pepper chopped
1 cup mayonnaise

1 cup sour cream
1 teaspoon curry powder
salt and pepper
8 hard rolls

This is an easy main dish for a summer buffet supper. Mix chicken, celery, and pepper. Mix mayonnaise, sour cream, and curry powder (add this to taste). Blend the two mixtures and add salt and pepper to taste. Cut tops from rolls, dig out most of the soft centers, and fill with salad. SERVES 8.

CHICKEN À LA KING

2 cups LO chicken meat,
    mostly white, cut in
    ½-inch dice
2 tablespoons butter or
    margarine
½ pound mushrooms sliced
    thin

2 small green peppers sliced
    thin
½ cup drained canned
    pimiento sliced
3 cups cream sauce
salt and pepper
3 small or 2 large egg yolks
pinch of nutmeg

Heat fat in heavy skillet and in it sauté very lightly the mushrooms and green peppers. Add pimiento and chicken and heat through. Make cream sauce with 4 tablespoons butter or margarine, 4 tablespoons flour, and either 3 cups of top milk or 2 cups of top milk and 1 cup chicken broth. Season to taste and beat in egg yolks, one at a time. Add nutmeg and chicken mixture. Reheat, but not to the boiling point. Serve in heated patty shells or on hot fluffy rice or over fresh toast.   SERVES 6.

CHICKEN WITH ALMONDS

2½ cups LO chicken diced
3 tablespoons butter or
    margarine
½ cup shredded green
    pepper
½ cup onion sliced thin
1 cup rich chicken broth

salt and pepper
1 teaspoon curry powder
1 tablespoon flour
1 cup blanched almonds
    slivered
½ cup sliced mushrooms
    lightly sautéed

Chicken and almonds have a natural affinity for each other, and this is one of several recipes to make the most of it.

Heat fat in a skillet and cook green pepper and onion lightly—not enough to color onions. Add chicken meat and simmer about 5 minutes, stirring frequently. Add chicken broth. (If you use canned broth boil it down considerably to condense it.) Season to taste with salt and pepper. Combine curry powder and flour and make a paste with a little cold chicken broth or water. Stir into chicken mixture, stirring constantly until smooth and thickened. Simmer gently, covered, about 10 minutes. Just before serving stir in almonds and mushrooms. Serve in patty shells, in bread cases (see recipe for Chicken Patties, p. 95), or on hot fluffy rice or buttered noodles.   SERVES 5–6.

CHICKEN-ALMOND-RICE CASSEROLE

2–3 cups LO diced chicken
2 cups LO boiled rice
2 cups chicken broth
4 tablespoons butter or
    margarine
4 tablespoons flour
2 cups milk
salt and pepper
1 tablespoon minced onion

pinch of ground ginger
¼ teaspoon nutmeg
1–1½ cups sliced mushrooms sautéed lightly
¾ cup blanched almonds slivered and toasted
2 cups buttered fresh bread crumbs
paprika

Pour half of the chicken broth over the rice, stir well, and let stand while preparing balance of casserole. Heat butter in skillet, blend in flour, cook a moment, and stir in both remaining cup of chicken broth and milk. Stir until smooth and let simmer until thickened. Season to taste, and stir in onion, ginger, and nutmeg. In a greased 2-quart casserole arrange layers of rice, chicken, cream sauce, mushrooms, and almonds. Repeat layers, using half of each ingredient for each layer. Arrange crumbs in thick layer on top, sprinkle with paprika, and bake at 300° for 35 minutes (or 25 minutes at 400° if you are in a hurry), or until well browned.   SERVES 6.

CHICKEN-ALMOND SCRAMBLED EGGS

½ cup finely chopped LO chicken

4 eggs lightly beaten with fork

4 tablespoons butter or margarine

½ cup blanched, toasted almonds rolled fine

1 medium onion minced

dash Tabasco sauce

½ teaspoon chili powder

½ cup light cream

¼ cup consommé

¼ cup dry white wine

salt and pepper

A very small amount of leftover chicken here helps to make scrambled eggs a glamorous supper dish. Of course the almonds and wine do their share too!

Melt butter in heavy skillet and add almonds, onion, Tabasco, chili powder, and chicken. Brown lightly, stirring frequently, and stir in cream, consommé, and wine. Cook until liquid is partially evaporated and then pour in eggs, season to taste, and stir gently until eggs are just set.

SERVES 4.

CHICKEN-ALMOND SOUFFLÉ

2 cups finely chopped LO chicken

4 tablespoons butter

½ small onion minced

4 tablespoons flour

2 cups milk or 1 cup milk and 1 cup chicken broth

¼ cup almonds, blanched, shredded and toasted

2 tablespoons finely chopped mushrooms

¼ cup bread crumbs

2 egg yolks slightly beaten

1 teaspoon chervil

1 teaspoon parsley minced

1 teaspoon chopped chives

3 egg whites beaten stiff

dash of nutmeg

Melt butter in skillet and cook onion until soft but not brown. Stir in flour, cook a moment, and blend in milk (or milk and chicken broth), stirring constantly until sauce is

thick and smooth. Season to taste and stir in chicken, almonds, mushrooms, bread crumbs, yolks of eggs, and herbs.
Cool to lukewarm. Fold in stiffly beaten egg whites to which
nutmeg has been added, and pour into well-greased 6-cup
casserole. Bake 30–35 minutes at 400°—about 10 minutes
longer if you want it firm all through. Knife inserted in center will come out clean if soufflé is firm.   SERVES 6.

CHICKEN-ALMOND MOUSSE

½–¾ cup LO chicken minced
3 egg yolks slightly beaten
¼ teaspoon salt
¼ teaspoon celery salt
¼ teaspoon paprika
1 cup hot chicken broth
1 envelope unflavored
    gelatin
¼ cup cold water

½ cup chopped or slivered
    almonds, blanched and
    toasted
½ cup seedless white grapes
    (opt.)
½ teaspoon grated onion
1 cup heavy cream
    whipped
4 tablespoons dry sherry

Combine egg yolks, salt, celery salt, and paprika in top of
double boiler. Gradually pour on hot broth and cook over
hot water until thickened, stirring constantly. Soften gelatin
in water and add, stirring until dissolved. Remove from heat
and add chicken, nuts, grapes, and onion. Cool to lukewarm
and fold in whipped cream and sherry. Pour into mold or
ring mold rinsed in cold water and chill until firm. Unmold
on chilled platter. Surround with crisp watercress and in the
center of the ring, or in a separate bowl, serve mayonnaise
blended with a little sour cream and a little curry powder.
    SERVES 5–6.

QUICK CHICKEN-ASPARAGUS CASSEROLE

LO chicken sliced
1 pound cooked asparagus
    spears, fresh or frozen
1 can condensed cream of
    chicken soup
¼ cup heavy cream

salt and pepper
½ cup grated Parmesan
    cheese
1 tablespoon butter
paprika

This is a simple and good substitute for the elaborate and delicious Chicken Parisienne.

Place cooked asparagus in a layer on the bottom of a well-greased flat-bottomed casserole, preferably shallow. Lay chicken slices on top, overlapping them if you have plenty of chicken. In a saucepan mix soup, cream, seasoning, and half of the cheese. Cook over low heat until smooth and well blended, stirring constantly. Pour sauce over the chicken slices, masking completely. Top with remaining cheese, dot with butter, sprinkle lightly with paprika, and bake in hot oven, 450°, until golden brown on top, about 15 minutes.   SERVES 4.

CHICKEN-BISCUIT ROLLS

1¼ cups LO chicken diced
⅓ cup chopped ripe olives
⅛ teaspoon minced onion
1 teaspoon pimiento minced

⅛ teaspoon paprika
½ cup chicken gravy or
    cream sauce
biscuit dough (½ recipe)

Combine chicken, olives, onion, pimiento, and paprika, and add just enough gravy or cream sauce to hold it together. Make your favorite biscuit recipe. Roll or pat dough to a thickness of ¼ inch on a floured board, keeping the shape rectangular, about 8 x 10 inches. Spread chicken mixture over the top and roll up like a jelly roll. If you put the dough on a pastry cloth or waxed paper, you can roll it easily by lifting the cloth or paper as you roll. Cut with a sharp knife in 1-inch pieces, laying them close together in shallow greased casserole. Bake 15–20 minutes in a hot oven, 425°. Serve with plenty of chicken gravy or rich cream sauce.   SERVES 4–5.

CHICKEN CREOLE JAMBALAYA

3 cups LO chicken diced
3 slices bacon diced
1 clove garlic mashed
2 large onions chopped
3 stalks celery chopped
1 tablespoon chopped parsley
1 large green pepper chopped

1 tablespoon flour
2 cups canned tomatoes
1 teaspoon sweet basil
salt and pepper
dash of nutmeg
1½ cups cooked rice (LO if you have it)
½ cup buttered bread crumbs

Cook bacon in large skillet and when it is partially done add garlic, onions, celery, parsley, and green pepper, and cook until onion is yellow, stirring occasionally. Stir in flour, let simmer a moment, and add tomatoes, basil, salt and pepper to taste, and nutmeg. Stir in rice and chicken, turn into 2-quart casserole, cover with crumbs, and bake in 350° oven 45 minutes to an hour. If crumbs brown sooner cover casserole with buttered brown paper or aluminum foil for a time.   SERVES 8.

CHICKEN (OR TURKEY) NEWBURG

3 *cups LO chicken cut in*
  large dice
1 *tablespoon butter or*
  margarine
1 *small onion minced*
½ *cup dry white wine*
2 *cups white sauce made*
  with 1 cup top milk and
  1 *cup chicken broth*
  boiled down to
  condense

salt and pepper
⅛ *teaspoon nutmeg*
½ *cup blanched almonds*
  slivered and toasted
2 *egg yolks lightly beaten*
½ *cup light cream*
¼ *cup sherry*

Melt butter in skillet and sauté onion until soft and transparent looking. Stir in wine and add to white sauce, which
has been made with 3 tablespoons butter or margarine, 3
tablespoons flour, and the liquid listed above. Stir until
smooth, season to taste with salt, pepper, and nutmeg, and
turn into top of double boiler. Add chicken and cook over
boiling water 20–25 minutes. Add almonds. Blend egg
yolks and cream and stir quickly into chicken mixture, stirring constantly until smooth and thick. Add sherry and
serve at once over fluffy rice, buttered noodles, fresh hot
cornbread split and buttered, or buttered toast. SERVES 6.

CHICKEN CROQUETTES

2 *cups LO chicken meat*
  chopped fine or ground
  coarsely
1 *cup chicken broth*
½ *tablespoon butter*
½ *tablespoon flour*
¼ *cup chopped nuts*
1 *teaspoon lemon juice*

1 *teaspoon onion juice or*
  grated onion
1 *tablespoon minced*
  parsley
salt to taste
chili powder to taste
3 *eggs*
fine bread crumbs
fat for deep frying

Heat chicken broth in a saucepan. While it is heating knead

butter and flour to a paste. Add to hot broth and stir constantly until broth is smooth and thickened. Cook 3–4 minutes over low heat and strain through a fine sieve. Reheat over low heat and stir in chicken meat, nuts, lemon juice, onion juice, parsley, salt to taste, and enough chili powder to give mixture a slight tang—½–¾ teaspoon is usually enough. Remove from stove and beat in 2 eggs, one at a time, beating vigorously. Spread mixture on cold platter and chill. Then take up mixture by large spoonfuls and mold into croquettes—cone-shaped, pear-shaped, or sausage-shaped. Dip first into fine crumbs, then in egg beaten lightly with a spoonful or so of water, and again into crumbs. Chill again. At dinnertime fry in deep fat at 390° until golden brown all over. Drain on brown paper or absorbent paper toweling and keep hot until all are ready. Serve with rich cream sauce or mushroom sauce.   SERVES 4–5.

CHICKEN-MACARONI CASSEROLE MEAL

2 cups LO chicken diced	salt and pepper
1 cup LO chicken gravy	½ teaspoon chopped parsley
¾ cup whole-kernel corn	2 cups cooked macaroni,
2 tablespoons green pepper	spaghetti, or noodles
chopped fine	1 tablespoon butter
¼ cup mushrooms chopped	2 tablespoons grated
	Parmesan cheese

Mix the chicken, gravy (thinned with a little milk if it is very thick), corn, green pepper, mushrooms, salt and pepper to taste, and parsley. Pour into a 6-cup casserole and arrange the macaroni, spaghetti, or noodles on top. Dot with butter and sprinkle with cheese. Cover and bake in moderate oven, 350°, 30 minutes, or until bubbly. Remove cover last 10 minutes.   SERVES 4–5.

CHICKEN-MUSHROOM SOUFFLÉ

1 cup LO chicken diced
    small
3 tablespoons butter
3 tablespoons flour
½ cup milk
½ cup condensed cream of
    mushroom soup

salt and pepper
1 teaspoon parsley minced
1 teaspoon finely cut chives
dash of paprika
3 eggs separated

Melt butter in skillet, stir in flour, cook a moment, and add gradually milk and soup, stirring until smooth and thick. Season to taste, let simmer a few minutes, and mix in chicken, parsley, chives, paprika, and well-beaten egg yolks. Cool to lukewarm, beat egg whites until stiff but not dry, and fold in gently. Turn into small greased casserole and bake in moderate oven, 350°, for 35–45 minutes, or until soufflé is as firm as you want it.   SERVES 4.

CHICKEN PATTIES

1–1½ cups LO white meat
    of chicken cut in
    ½-inch dice
½ cup cooked sweetbread
    diced (opt.)
2 cups cream sauce
2 egg yolks

¼ cup sliced mushrooms
    cooked in a little water
3 tablespoons heavy cream
¼ cup dry sherry
salt and pepper to taste
patty shells

Make the cream sauce with 3 tablespoons butter or margarine, 3 tablespoons flour, and 2 cups whole milk. Add to it 2 tablespoons of the water in which mushrooms were cooked. Stir egg yolks and cream together with a fork until blended and add to cream sauce.

In another pan combine chicken, sweetbread, mushrooms, and sherry and heat through, stirring occasionally. Stir in cream sauce and season to taste. If you are not ready to serve at once, keep mixture hot in a double boiler, *not* on direct heat. Serve in patty shells made from pastry or bread cases. To make the latter, cut 2-inch slices of bread into good-sized circles or squares, remove centers, brush with melted butter, and brown in hot oven, 400°.

This recipe will serve 4–5, depending on size of patties.

CHICKEN AND EGG PATTIES

1½ *cups minced LO chicken*   ½ *teaspoon Worcestershire*
    (*or turkey*)   *sauce*
4 *3-inch bread cubes*   2 *tablespoons grated*
4 *eggs*   *Parmesan cheese*
2 *cups cream sauce*   1 *tablespoon grated Swiss*
salt and pepper   *cheese*

Hollow out bread cubes so that only a shell is left, ¼–⅜ inch thick. Toast shells in oven, turning to be sure they are browned on all sides.

Make cream sauce of 3 tablespoons butter or margarine, 3 tablespoons flour, and 2 cups top milk. Season to taste and divide into two saucepans. To one add chicken and Worcestershire sauce, and simmer a few moments. To the other add both Parmesan and Swiss cheese, stirring until cheese is melted. While preparing cream sauce, poach the eggs. Lay bread cases in shallow casserole or heat-proof platter, fill with chicken mixture, lay poached eggs on top, and cover with cheese sauce. Brown lightly under broiler.

SERVES 4.

CHICKEN-PANCAKE ROLLS

1 *cup LO chicken chopped*	¼ *cup chopped mushrooms*
1 *tablespoon butter*	*sautéed*
2 *teaspoons flour*	1 *recipe pancake batter*
½ *cup light cream*	*sour cream*
salt and pepper	¼ *cup grated cheese*
¼ *cup chopped almonds*	2 *tablespoons butter*

Here is another wonderful way to use leftover chicken, and the best part of it is that it can be made well in advance— the pancakes are just as good when the casserole is heated as they are fresh.

Melt butter in skillet, blend in flour, cook a minute, and add cream gradually, stirring until sauce is smooth and thick. Season to taste and let simmer a minute. Add chicken, mushrooms, and almonds, and mix well.

Use your favorite pancake batter to make the pancakes. They should be quite rich and tender. If you use a prepared mix add some extra melted shortening, a tablespoon of brown sugar, and one egg beaten lightly. Make rather large pancakes. As each is done, put a tablespoon of the chicken mixture on it, roll up, and arrange side by side in a well-greased shallow casserole, packed close together. Put a teaspoon of sour cream on top of each roll, sprinkle cheese over all, dot with butter, and bake at 375° 20 minutes.

SERVES 6.

CHICKEN-NOODLE CASSEROLE

2 *cups LO chicken diced*
½ *pound medium noodles*
3 *tablespoons butter*
3 *tablespoons flour*
1½ *cups light cream*
1½ *cups chicken stock*
2 *egg yolks beaten slightly*

1 *cup sliced mushrooms*
   sautéed (opt.)
2 *tablespoons chopped*
   green pepper sautéed
   (opt.)
salt and pepper to taste
2 *tablespoons sherry (opt.)*
butter and Parmesan cheese
for top

Cook noodles in boiling salted water until tender (about 7 minutes). Drain, rinse in cold water, and drain again. Melt butter in skillet, stir in flour, blend in cream and chicken stock (canned will do), and stir until smooth. Remove from fire, mix a little with egg yolks, and stir into sauce. Mix everything together—noodles, chicken meat, sauce, mushrooms, green pepper, seasonings, and sherry—and pour into large greased casserole. Top with butter and grated Parmesan cheese. Bake at 350° for 20–25 minutes, or until top is golden brown.   SERVES 6.

CHICKEN PIE

2 *cups LO chicken cut in*
   rather large pieces
2 *cups chicken broth*
3 *tablespoons flour*
3 *tablespoons butter*
½ *cup cream*
¾ *cup cooked green peas*

½ *cup diced celery (opt.)*
½ *cup thinly sliced carrots*
   (opt.)
1 *cup potato balls (opt.)*
½ *cup mushrooms sautéed*
   (opt.)
pastry or biscuit dough

Bring chicken broth to a boil and stir in flour and butter kneaded to a smooth paste, stirring constantly until broth is thick and smooth. Lower heat, stir in cream, chicken, and vegetables, and heat through. Pour in 2-quart casserole and top with either small biscuits or pie crust rolled out and slashed several times to let steam escape. Bake at 450° about 20 minutes, or until top is well browned. SERVES 5–6.

CHICKEN PIE WITH CORN-MEAL MUSH TOP

I. The Casserole
2 cups coarsely diced LO chicken
2 sweetbreads cooked and diced (opt.)
3 tablespoons flour
5 tablespoons butter
2 artichoke bottoms quartered (canned, opt.)
½ teaspoon chopped parsley

1 pint light cream
3 ounces sherry (opt.)
salt and pepper

II. Corn-meal Mush
2 cups water
1½ teaspoons salt
½ cup corn meal (preferably water-ground)

If you want to stretch a limited amount of leftover chicken, sweetbreads will answer the purpose well.

If you like the flavor of corn-meal mush, this chicken pie is both unusual and very good. Make the mush the day before. Add salt to water and bring to a hard boil in the top of a double boiler over direct heat. Reduce heat and add corn meal slowly, stirring rapidly as it thickens. Move to bottom part of double boiler and let it cook over boiling water, covered, 30 minutes. Spread on a well-greased pie plate large enough so that the mush is about ½ inch thick. Chill overnight. If you want a lighter-textured mush, beat batter several minutes before you pour it out, preferably in an electric mixer.

To cook the sweetbreads, plunge them in cold water as soon as you get them and let them stand an hour. Drain, cover with boiling water and 1 teaspoon salt and 2 tablespoons lemon juice or vinegar per quart of water. Simmer 20 minutes, drain, and plunge into cold water. When cold remove membranes and tubes and dice.

Put flour in a paper bag and shake sweetbread pieces in it. Sprinkle remaining flour over chicken. Melt 3 table-

spoons of the butter in a heavy skillet and lightly brown
chicken and sweetbreads in it. Transfer to 2-quart casserole,
add the artichoke bottoms, and sprinkle with parsley. Pour
cream into the skillet in which you browned the chicken
and cook a few minutes over fairly high heat, stirring constantly and scraping up all the glaze. Add sherry and pour
into casserole.

Spread the cold corn-meal mush with the remaining butter, cut into rather small squares or diamonds, and arrange
over top of casserole. Bake 20 minutes in a 400° oven. If
the top has not browned then put it under the broiler a few
minutes.   SERVES 6.

CHICKEN OR TURKEY TETRAZZINI

2 cups LO chicken or
    turkey cut in ½-inch
    dice
¼ pound butter (preferably
    sweet)
¼ pound mushrooms sliced
    thin
1 pint heavy cream
1 tablespoon sherry (opt.)

2 tablespoons dry white
    wine (opt.)
salt and pepper
2 tablespoons flour
2 tablespoons butter
¼ pound medium noodles
    or thin spaghetti
3 tablespoons grated
    Parmesan cheese

Melt the ¼ pound butter in skillet and sauté mushrooms 2–3
minutes. Add chicken meat, cream, wine, season to taste,
and heat almost to boiling. Knead flour and 2 tablespoons
butter together to a smooth paste and stir into the chicken
mixture, continuing to stir until smooth and somewhat
thickened. Let simmer about 5 minutes.

In the meantime, cook spaghetti or noodles in boiling
salted water until just tender, 7–10 minutes. Drain, rinse in
cold water, and spread on bottom of rather shallow greased
casserole. Pour the chicken-mushroom mixture gently over
it, sprinkle with Parmesan cheese, and bake in a 375° oven
about 20 minutes, or until top is golden brown. If you are
making it just at serving time so that all ingredients are hot,
merely slide it under the broiler and brown.   SERVES 4.

CHICKEN PUDDING

LO chicken in large pieces   *4 eggs well beaten*
1½ cups chicken broth   *salt and pepper*
1 cup light cream scalded   *dash of cayenne*

This chicken "custard" is a very delicate dish. It can be made with any quantity of chicken, but the amounts given here for custard would call for about half of a roast chicken.

Break up chicken in as large pieces as possible, removing bones. Arrange in casserole. Heat broth and combine with scalded cream. Pour gradually over eggs, stirring vigorously to prevent eggs from "setting." Season to taste, pour over chicken, and bake 50–60 minutes in a moderate oven, 350°, or until custard is firm to the touch and top browned. Serves 4–6, depending upon amount of chicken you start with.

CHICKEN TIMBALES

1½ cups LO chicken ground   *salt and pepper*
3 tablespoons butter or   *pinch of thyme*
*   margarine*   *2 eggs separated*
⅛ cup fine bread crumbs   *1 pimiento chopped*
1 cup light cream   *   (canned)*

Melt butter in saucepan, stir in bread crumbs, cook for a moment, and gradually stir in cream. Season with salt and pepper and thyme and cook until smooth, stirring constantly. Remove from heat and beat in egg yolks, one at a time. Cook a moment more, and stir in chicken and pimiento. Cool a little and fold in stiffly beaten egg whites. Put in well-greased shallow mold or 6 individual molds, set in pan of hot water, and bake 25 minutes in moderate oven, 350°, or until firm to the touch. The large mold will take a little longer than the small ones. Unmold on hot platter and surround with either mushroom sauce, tomato sauce, or a plain rich cream sauce.   SERVES 6.

CHICKEN SHORTCAKE

1½ cups LO cooked chicken cut in ½-inch dice	1½ cups chicken broth
3 tablespoons chicken fat, butter, or margarine	½ cup sliced mushrooms sautéed lightly
3 tablespoons flour	salt and pepper
	baking-powder biscuits

Heat fat in top of double boiler over boiling water, blend in flour, add chicken broth slowly, and cook until smooth and thick, stirring frequently. Add chicken and mushrooms, season to taste, and continue to cook 10–15 minutes.

Bake your favorite biscuits, cutting them rather large and rolling or patting them about ¾ inch thick. Bake 12–15 minutes in 450° oven, split, and butter generously. Cover bottom half with creamed chicken, replace top half, and add more chicken.   SERVES 4–5.

CHICKEN TURNOVERS

1 cup ground or minced LO chicken	¼ cup chopped stuffed olives
6 slices white bread, crusts removed	¼ teaspoon rosemary
1 egg yolk lightly beaten	⅛ teaspoon ground ginger
1 small clove garlic mashed	1 tablespoon lemon juice
2 tablespoons chopped onion	dash Tabasco
1 tablespoon chopped parsley	salt and pepper
	pastry for 2-crust pie

These flavorsome turnovers are simple to make, and are good either with cocktails, in miniature sizes, or as a main course, served with a rich cream sauce or mushroom sauce.

Cover bread with water, let stand a moment, and then squeeze out water. Mash, mix with chicken, egg yolk, garlic, onion, parsley, olives, and seasonings. Roll out your favorite pastry a little less than ⅛ inch thick. Cut in 2-inch squares for cocktail snacks or 6-inch squares for luncheon turnovers. Divide filling among squares, placing in center. Fold into triangles. Brush lower edge with water, press together, and crimp the edges with a fork. Brush tops with milk, cream, or unbeaten egg white, and bake in hot oven, 400°, 8–10 minutes for small turnovers, 12–15 minutes for large ones. This amount will make 6 or 7 large turnovers.

CREAMED CHICKEN AND OYSTERS

1½ cups LO chicken cut up
1 pint oysters with their
    liquor
3 tablespoons chicken fat or
    butter or margarine

3 tablespoons flour
1 cup chicken broth or milk
1 cup light cream
salt and pepper

A pint of oysters does a lot to make a delicious new dish out of the remains of a chicken. The combination of flavors is usually well liked.

Melt fat in heavy skillet, blend in flour, and gradually stir in chicken broth or milk and cream, stirring constantly until smooth and thick. Add chicken, and while it heats put oysters (well picked over) in a saucepan in their liquor and heat until the edges curl. Add to the chicken mixture and cook over low heat a moment. Season to taste. Serve over hot biscuits or hot cornbread, split and buttered.

SERVES 5–6.

CURRIED CHICKEN OR TURKEY

2 cups LO chicken or
    turkey sliced rather
    thin
1 tablespoon butter or
    margarine
2 tablespoons chopped
    onion
½ small bay leaf

pinch of thyme
1–2 tablespoons curry
    powder
½ cup chicken broth
1½ cups white sauce made
    with chicken broth
½ cup light cream

For people who like the exotic taste of curry, chicken curry is one of the most delightful ways to transform LO chicken (or turkey), and this is one of the simplest recipes for it.

Melt butter in saucepan and cook onion until it begins to take on color. Add bay leaf, thyme, curry powder, and ¼ cup chicken broth and stir until well blended. Make white sauce with 2 tablespoons butter or margarine, 2 tablespoons flour, and 1½ cups chicken broth. Season to taste, add to curry mixture, stir until smooth, and let simmer 10–15 minutes. Meantime, cover chicken or turkey slices with remaining ¼ cup chicken broth and heat through. Add to the curry sauce, correct seasoning (adding more curry powder if you like it strong), and keep hot in a double boiler until ready to serve—the longer the better. Stir in cream just before serving. Serve with freshly boiled rice.

The traditional accompaniments of curry include chutney, fresh coconut (in pieces to eat by hand or grated to sprinkle over the top), chopped salted peanuts, preserved or candied ginger, poppadums (a large, thin wafer imported from India, to be fried in deep fat, but for which toasted and buttered pilot crackers make an adequate substitute), and Bombay duck, a dried, salted fish also imported from India, for which finely shredded dried codfish makes an acceptable substitute.   SERVES 4.

DEVILED CHICKEN BALLS

1½ cups LO chicken minced
2 tablespoons chopped
    chives
1 tablespoon minced
    parsley
2 tablespoons finely
    chopped celery
2 tablespoons bread crumbs

1 tablespoon grated onion
1 tablespoon curry powder
    (scant)
prepared mustard
salt
fine bread crumbs
1 egg
fat for deep frying

Made small, the size of a medium olive, these balls are a
good hot hors d'oeuvre. Made the size of a small egg they
make a good hot dish for a light meal.

Mix well chicken, chives, parsley, celery, bread crumbs,
onion, and curry powder. Add just enough prepared mustard to hold the mixture together. Salt to taste. Shape into
balls, roll in fine bread crumbs, then in egg beaten lightly
with a tablespoon or so of water, and again in fine crumbs.
Chill. When ready to serve fry in deep fat at 385° until
golden brown all over. Drain on brown paper or paper
towels. If served as hors d'oeuvres stick a toothpick in each
one. In either case serve with hot tomato sauce. SERVES 4.

JAPANESE CHICKEN

2 cups LO chicken cut in
    julienne strips
2 cups LO boiled rice
1 clove of garlic
2 tablespoons butter or
    margarine

2 tablespoons flour
1 cup chicken broth
1 teaspoon soy sauce
salt and pepper

This is an unusually simple and delicious combination of
leftover chicken and leftover rice.

Make this dish in a heavy casserole in which it can be

served. Rub it well with the cut clove of garlic and melt butter in it. Blend in flour and chicken broth. When it is smooth and thick, add soy sauce, chicken, and salt and pepper to taste. Spread the rice over the top, cover tightly, and cook over lowest possible heat 5–6 minutes, just enough to heat the rice through.   SERVES 4–5.

VIRGINIA CHICKEN

2 cups LO cooked chicken cut in ½-inch dice

2 tablespoons LO cooked ham chopped (opt.)

2 small-medium tomatoes peeled and chopped

2 shallots or 1 small onion chopped

2 tablespoons chopped green pepper

1 cup corn (LO, cut from cob, frozen or canned)

½ cup cooked okra (opt.)

1 cup LO baby lima beans

3 tablespoons butter or margarine

salt and pepper

With the proper combination of leftover vegetables here, a little chicken can go a long way toward providing a whole meal, and a good one. It is also good cold as a hot-weather meal.

Put the chicken, ham, and vegetables in a bowl and mix lightly. Melt butter in skillet, turn in chicken-vegetable mixture, and heat over a low flame until very hot, stirring gently frequently. Season to taste.   SERVES 4–5.

YANKEE CHICKEN HASH

2 cups coarsely chopped
    LO chicken
1 cup LO cooked sausage
    meat or 1 small can
    Vienna sausages
    chopped
½ cup chopped green
    pepper
½ cup chopped onion
2 tablespoons chopped
    parsley

1 tablespoon chopped
    chives
½ cup coarse bread crumbs
½ teaspoon grated lemon
    rind
½ cup rich cream sauce or
    gravy
salt and pepper
4 tablespoons butter or
    margarine

The quickest way to make this hash is to put chicken, sausage, green pepper, onion, parsley, and chives in a large wooden chopping bowl and chop them to quite small pieces. Stir in bread crumbs, lemon rind, and cream sauce, made with 1 tablespoon butter or margarine, 1 tablespoon flour, and ½ cup top milk, with seasoning to taste. Chicken gravy is even better if you have it left over. Season mixture to taste. Heat fat in heavy skillet and spread hash evenly. Cook gently over low heat until bottom is brown and crusty. Fold in half and slide onto hot platter.   SERVES 5–6.

CHINESE CHICKEN SALAD

2 cups LO chicken cut fine
    but not ground
2 tablespoons unflavored
    gelatin
¼ cup cold water
1½ cups boiling chicken
    stock

1 cup pineapple juice
salt
½ teaspoon paprika
1½ cups drained sliced
    pineapple cut in pieces
¾ cup almonds blanched,
    slivered, and toasted

Soften gelatin in cold water and dissolve in hot chicken stock. (If you use canned chicken broth boil it down to condense it somewhat.) Blend with pineapple juice, salt to taste, and paprika. Chill until somewhat thick but not set. Rinse mold in cold water and arrange chicken, pineapple, and almonds in it. Pour chilled mixture over and chill until firm. Unmold on chilled platter and serve with mayonnaise.

SERVES 6.

HEARTY CHICKEN SALAD

1–1½ cups LO chicken sliced and cut in medium pieces

1 cup LO cauliflower flowerets

1 cup LO string beans cut in pieces or julienned

2 small tomatoes peeled, seeded, and chopped coarsely

2 hard-cooked eggs

¼ cup French dressing

½ teaspoon minced parsley

½ teaspoon chopped chives

Put in a bowl chicken pieces, cauliflower, string beans, and tomatoes. Cut eggs in two, remove yolks to a small bowl, chop whites, and add to chicken-vegetable mixture. Mash yolks and blend into French dressing. Toss salad mixture lightly with the dressing. Sprinkle top with parsley and chives mixed.

SERVES 5–6.

RUSSIAN CHICKEN SALAD

1½ cups white meat of LO chicken cut in julienne strips

3 small boiled potatoes, peeled and sliced thin

2 tablespoons thin slices of dill pickle

3 tablespoons mayonnaise

1 teaspoon Worcestershire sauce

Blend mayonnaise and Worcestershire sauce, and combine gently with remaining ingredients. Arrange on lettuce-lined serving dish, and garnish with wedges of hard-cooked eggs and tomatoes.

SERVES 4.

SINGAPORE SALAD

3 cups LO chicken cut in
    julienne strips
cut clove of garlic
1 small head lettuce
    shredded
1 green pepper shredded
1 sweet red pepper
    shredded
3 stalks celery chopped
1 cup mayonnaise
juice ½ lemon

3 tablespoons Major Grey's
    chutney chopped
    coarsely
1 tablespoon Madeira or
    sherry
1 tablespoon chopped
    chives
1 teaspoon salt
1 teaspoon Worcestershire
    sauce
½ teaspoon paprika
dash cayenne pepper

This is a most unusual chicken salad, spicy and fragrant, a
fine company dish. It can also be made with LO turkey or
ham.

Rub a wooden salad bowl with the cut clove of garlic, and
put in the bowl the lettuce, green and red pepper (no
seeds), celery, and chicken. In another bowl mix well all
the remaining ingredients and blend lightly but thoroughly
with the salad.   SERVES 6.

TEXAS CHICKEN SALAD

2 cups LO chicken meat
    cut in small dice
½ cup chopped celery
½ cup shredded green
    pepper
½ cup cucumber diced
    small
1 cup grapefruit sections,
    preferably pink

½ cup French dressing
½ cup mayonnaise
1 teaspoon curry powder
1 tablespoon grated onion
1 tablespoon minced
    parsley
1 tablespoon chopped
    chives
paprika

This is an unusual chicken salad, both flavor and texture
being added by the cucumber, grapefruit, and curry.

Mix lightly the chicken meat, celery, green pepper, cucumber, grapefruit sections (cut in two or three pieces if large), and French dressing. Chill until serving time. In the meantime blend mayonnaise with curry powder, onion, half of the parsley, and chives. Let stand. When ready to serve, press any excess dressing out of salad, mix with mayonnaise, spoon over crisp lettuce leaves or a bed of crisp watercress on a platter, and sprinkle with remaining parsley and with paprika.   SERVES 6.

DUCK

DUCK SOUP

carcasses of 2 medium roast   1 carrot coarsely sliced
    ducks   1 teaspoon minced parsley
7 cups water   1½–2 cups LO boiled rice
2–3 stalks of celery cut up   salt and pepper

Break up the duck carcasses, smashing larger bones with
cleaver or hammer. Put in soup kettle with water, celery,
carrot, and parsley. Heat to boiling, reduce heat, remove
scum that comes to the top, cover, and simmer about 2
hours. Strain. Skim off excess fat, add any bits of duck meat
you can salvage, season to taste, stir in rice, and reheat
slowly. Serves 7–10, depending upon whether served in
cups or soup bowls.

HOT DUCK OPEN SANDWICHES

2 cups LO duck cut up   ⅓ cup cream
¼ cup butter   salt and pepper
1 egg well beaten

Melt butter in heavy skillet and cook duck in it 2–3 minutes, stirring constantly. Blend egg and cream well, add to
duck, and cook slowly, stirring gently but constantly until
thickened. Serve on fresh buttered toast, French toast, or
waffles.   SERVES 4.

DUCK SANDWICHES

thin slices LO duck   ¼ *cup mayonnaise*
1 *cup raisins ground*   1 *teaspoon lemon juice*

Mix raisins, mayonnaise, and lemon juice. Spread rather thick on buttered slices of bread and top with slices of duck. This amount will spread 8–10 slices.

DUCK À LA KING

1 *cup diced LO cooked*   3 *tablespoons flour*
   duck   1¾ *cups milk*
2 *tablespoons duck fat,*   *salt and pepper*
   butter, or margarine   *pinch sweet marjoram*
2 *tablespoons chopped*   2 *teaspoons lemon juice*
   onion   1 *egg well beaten*
1 *cup coarsely chopped*
   mushrooms

Roast duck is hard to carve economically at the table, and a little time and energy devoted to the carcass afterward can usually salvage enough small pieces of duck to provide another meal. Here is a good recipe for using the scraps.

Heat fat in heavy skillet and cook onion and mushrooms until onion is slightly yellow. Blend in flour, cook until smooth, and gradually stir in milk. Continue stirring until sauce is smooth and thickened. Add salt and pepper to taste, marjoram, lemon juice, and duck meat. Heat thoroughly, and spoon out a little of the sauce to add to the egg. Stir quickly into the mixture and cook only until well heated. Serve at once over hot fluffy rice, hot buttered noodles, or fresh hot cornbread split and buttered. SERVES 4.

DUCK TIMBALES

1 *cup LO duck meat*
   ground
1 *cup soft bread crumbs*
¾ *cup milk*
2 *tablespoons sherry*
1 *teaspoon minced parsley*

1 *teaspoon minced shallot*
   or onion
salt and pepper
½ *teaspoon nutmeg*
3 *egg whites beaten stiff*

If you can salvage as much as a cup of scraps from the duck carcass this is a wonderful way to make a fine meal of them.

Mix milk and crumbs in a saucepan and cook over low heat 4–5 minutes. While it is cooking pour sherry over duck meat and let stand. Then mix crumb mixture, shallot, parsley, duck meat, and seasonings. Gently fold in egg whites. Turn into 6 well-buttered individual casseroles, a single rather shallow mold, or a ring mold. Set in pan of hot water and bake 30 minutes in moderate oven, 375°, or until top is firm to the touch. A single mold will take a little longer than individual molds. Let stand a moment when you remove them from the oven and unmold on heated platter. Surround with mushroom sauce or creamed spinach.

SERVES 6.

DUCK TURNOVERS

1½ *cups LO duck chopped*
1 *recipe pastry*
pinch nutmeg
pinch thyme
pinch powdered cloves
1 *tablespoon chopped*
   parsley

1 *tablespoon chopped*
   chives
1 *tablespoon chopped*
   onion
3 *tablespoons duck gravy*
   or rich cream sauce

If you have roasted two ducks for dinner you are almost certain to be able to get 1½ cups of scraps when you clean off the carcasses carefully. This recipe makes a second delicious meal from them.

Make your pastry first, sifting nutmeg, thyme, and cloves with the flour. Chill the dough while you prepare the filling for the turnovers. Add parsley, chives, and onion to chopped duck, mix well, and blend in gravy or cream sauce —just enough to hold the mixture together.

Roll out pastry to about ⅛ inch in thickness and in the shape of a rectangle. Cut in 6 squares. Divide the duck mixture among the squares, putting it in the center of each. Fold over into triangles, moisten the edges with cold water, and pinch together with a fork. Brush tops with an egg yolk beaten with 1 tablespoon milk, or with plain milk or cream. Bake 12–15 minutes in a hot oven, 425°.   SERVES 6.

HAWAIIAN DUCK

2 *cups LO duck cut in julienne strips*
3 *tablespoons butter or margarine*
1 *cup sliced onions*
1 *cup sliced celery*
2 *cups duck or chicken broth*
2 *tablespoons cornstarch*
3 *tablespoons soy sauce*
1 *cup shredded coconut*
1 *cup sliced mushrooms sautéed*
½ *teaspoon ground ginger*
salt and pepper

Heat butter in large heavy skillet and cook onion until soft but not colored. Add celery and cook 2–3 minutes longer. Add broth and heat to boiling. Mix cornstarch to a thin paste with water and stir into broth, stirring constantly until smooth and thickened. Season to taste with salt and pepper, add ginger, and stir in coconut, mushrooms, duck, and soy sauce. Cover and simmer over lowest possible heat about 10 minutes. Serve over fresh buttered toast, buttered noodles, hot fluffy rice, or hot cornbread split and buttered.
SERVES 6–8.

MADRAS DUCK SALAD

2 cups LO duck diced
1 tablespoon tarragon
    vinegar
½ teaspoon grated onion or
    onion juice
½ teaspoon dry mustard
¼ cup mayonnaise
¾ cup sour cream

¼ cup Indian chutney,
    preferably Major
    Grey's
salt and pepper
½ teaspoon paprika
1 medium avocado diced
1 large orange peeled,
    sliced ¼ inch thick, and
    cut in bite-size pieces

This combination of ingredients makes such an outstanding salad for anyone who likes really flavorful foods that it justifies roasting an extra duck for it when you are having roast duck.

Make the dressing first. Blend vinegar, onion, and mustard into a smooth paste. Blend with mayonnaise, sour cream, and chutney. Season with salt and pepper to taste, add paprika, and let stand until an hour before serving time. Then blend gently but thoroughly with duck, avocado, and orange. Chill. Serve on bed of crisp lettuce, garnished with watercress.   SERVES 5–6.

GOOSE

SECOND-DAY GOOSE

sliced LO goose
½ cup LO gravy thinned
    out or chicken broth
1 teaspoon grated orange
    rind

3 tablespoons currant jelly
½ cup seedless raisins
    parboiled

Slice off enough goose to make 6 portions. In a large skillet mix gravy or broth, orange rind, currant jelly, and plumped raisins. Heat to just under boiling, and when jelly is dissolved lay in slices of goose. Cover, reduce heat, and cook just long enough to heat goose thoroughly.

TURKEY

TURKEY SOUP

turkey carcass
1 bay leaf
½ teaspoon marjoram
½ teaspoon thyme
½ teaspoon basil
2 tablespoons butter or
    margarine
3 tablespoons flour

1 medium onion chopped
    fine
½ cup minced celery
salt and pepper
¼ cup raw rice
½ pound mushrooms sliced
    and sautéed
3 tablespoons Madeira or
    sherry

Here is the traditional last appearance of the turkey, and a delicious one it can be. To avoid keeping the turkey carcass on hand for several days, remove all usable meat from it as soon as possible and make the basic broth for turkey soup immediately.

Break up the carcass, cracking larger bones with a cleaver or hammer. Put in a large soup pot with bay leaf and other herbs, and enough water to cover completely, and simmer slowly, covered, for 3–4 hours. Strain through a fine sieve so as to remove little slivers of bone, and sort out pieces of turkey and put back in the broth. (At this stage broth can be stored to make soup another day.)

Melt butter in kettle large enough to hold the broth you have and blend in flour. Cook for a moment and then stir in stock gradually. Bring to boil and add onion, celery, rice, and seasoning to taste. Simmer until rice is soft—25–30 minutes—and add mushrooms. Just before serving add Madeira or sherry. Serves up to 10–12.

CREAMED TURKEY DE LUXE

2 cups LO turkey diced
1 tablespoon butter or
    margarine
1 tablespoon grated or
    minced onion
1 tablespoon chopped
    parsley

2 tablespoons LO gravy
pinch nutmeg
salt and pepper
1½ cups cream sauce
2 eggs beaten lightly
¼ cup sherry

The addition of beaten eggs to the cream sauce makes this dish outstanding in flavor.

Melt butter in a skillet and lightly sauté onion and parsley. Stir in turkey, gravy, nutmeg, and salt and pepper to taste. Keep warm while you make cream sauce, using 1½ tablespoons butter or margarine, 1½ tablespoons flour, and 1½ cups top milk or half cream, half milk. Stir constantly until smooth and thickened, season to taste, and quickly stir in eggs. Add turkey mixture, blend well, and add sherry. Serve at once, over hot fluffy rice, buttered noodles, or hot cornbread split and generously buttered.   SERVES 4–5.

SCALLOPED TURKEY

3 cups LO turkey diced
¾ cup turkey skin ground
2 cups LO turkey dressing
2 cups turkey broth
4 tablespoons butter or
    margarine
4 tablespoons flour

½ cup light cream
salt
½ teaspoon tarragon
½ teaspoon thyme
2 eggs lightly beaten
1 cup buttered bread
    crumbs

This rich casserole makes a fine main dish for a party. The ground turkey skin gives it special flavor.

Melt butter in heavy skillet, blend in flour, and gradually stir in turkey broth, obtained by boiling up the carcass as for soup. When sauce is thick and smooth add cream, salt, tarragon, and thyme. Let simmer about 5 minutes. Stir a little of the sauce into the eggs and add to sauce with ground skin. Remove from heat. Spread dressing evenly in bottom of well-greased 2-quart casserole. Pour over half the sauce. Add the turkey meat and the balance of the sauce. Top with buttered crumbs and bake in moderate oven, 350°, about 30 minutes, or until sauce is bubbling and crumbs well browned. SERVES 6.

TURKEY À LA REINE

2 cups diced LO turkey
yolks of 2 hard-cooked eggs
1 tablespoon butter or
    margarine
1 tablespoon flour
1 cup thinned-out turkey
    gravy or consommé
    (increase flour to 2
    tablespoons if you use
    consommé)
¼ cup dry Madeira or
    sherry

1 teaspoon Worcestershire
    sauce
1 teaspoon grated lemon
    rind
dash of nutmeg
salt and pepper
1 cup sliced mushrooms
    sautéed
1 tablespoon chopped
    parsley
whites of 2 hard-cooked
    eggs chopped

Mash egg yolks and butter to a smooth paste. Stir in flour, gravy, wine, Worcestershire sauce, lemon rind, and nutmeg. Cook 5 minutes over medium heat. Stir in turkey and mushrooms, turn into top of double boiler, and heat over boiling water 10–15 minutes. Turn out in serving dish and sprinkle with parsley and chopped whites of eggs. A nice last-minute touch, if you have them on hand, is the addition of 4 drained preserved chestnuts—marrons glacés.

SERVES 4.

TURKEY CROQUETTES

2 cups ground LO turkey
1½ tablespoons butter or
    margarine
1½ tablespoons minced
    onion
2 teaspoons minced parsley
2 teaspoons minced chives
pinch of mace

1½ tablespoons flour
½ cup top milk
2 egg yolks
fine crumbs or half crumbs
    and half ground
    blanched almonds
1 egg
fat for deep frying

Heat butter in skillet and cook onion until yellow. Stir in parsley, chives, mace, and flour, and cook until thick and smooth. Blend in milk and stir constantly until thick. Remove from stove and beat in egg yolks, one at a time. Stir in ground turkey and season to taste. Spread on a cold platter and chill. Then shape into croquettes by rolling between the palms (flour hands if it sticks). The croquettes can be cone-shaped, pear-shaped, or sausage-shaped. Roll in crumbs, then in egg beaten lightly with a few drops of water, and again in crumbs. Chill again. Fry a few at a time in hot deep fat at 390° until golden brown all over. Drain on brown paper or paper towels. Serve with a rich cream sauce or mushroom sauce.   SERVES 4–5.

TURKEY CASSEROLE

3 *cups LO turkey meat cut in small cubes*
4 *tablespoons butter or margarine*
3 *tablespoons flour*
1 *cup chicken stock*
3 *tablespoons sherry*
1 *cup light cream scalded*
1 *cup thinly sliced mushrooms sautéed*

pinch nutmeg
3 *egg yolks*
1 *tablespoon cold milk*
1 *teaspoon onion juice or grated onion*
1 *tablespoon minced green pepper*
bread crumbs
grated Parmesan cheese
salt and pepper

Heat 3 tablespoons of the butter in a skillet, cook the flour in it a moment, and gradually stir in chicken stock and sherry. When it reaches the boiling point lower heat, stir in cream and mushrooms, season to taste with salt and pepper, and add nutmeg. Beat egg yolks lightly with milk (with a fork) and quickly stir into sauce. Add onion, green pepper, and turkey meat. Turn into shallow greased casserole, sprinkle with bread crumbs and cheese, and dot with remaining tablespoon butter. Bake 15 minutes in hot oven, 425°. Casserole can also be browned under the broiler, but in this case reheat mixture after turkey is added.

SERVES 6–8.

TURKEY CASSEROLE WITH PEAS

2 *cups LO turkey diced small*
1 *cup LO turkey gravy turkey or chicken broth*
1 *teaspoon tomato sauce or catsup*

salt and pepper
1 *cup cooked green peas*
2 *tablespoons buttered crumbs*

Thin gravy with turkey or chicken broth until it has the consistency of cream. If you have no leftover gravy, make a sauce with 2 tablespoons butter or margarine, 2 tablespoons flour, and 1½ cups broth made by cooking turkey carcass as for soup. Add tomato sauce and season to taste. In greased quart casserole put half the turkey meat, then the peas, and the remainder of the turkey meat. Pour sauce over, top with buttered crumbs, and bake in hot oven, 400°, 20 minutes.   SERVES 4.

TURKEY-BROCCOLI CASSEROLE

2 cups LO turkey diced
    coarsely
1 package frozen broccoli or
    1 small bunch fresh
¼ pound medium-width
    noodles
2 tablespoons butter or
    margarine

2 tablespoons flour
2 cups whole milk
salt and pepper
1 cup grated sharp cheese
¼ cup blanched, toasted,
    and slivered almonds
    (opt.)

Cook broccoli just tender. If frozen, cut off the larger stems and chop coarsely. If fresh, cut big stems off before cooking, cut each in several pieces, and chop coarsely when cooked. Cook noodles in plenty of boiling salted water for 7–8 minutes, drain, rinse in cold water, and drain again.

Melt butter in skillet, stir in flour, cook a moment, and gradually stir in milk. Season to taste, add cheese, and simmer over very low heat until cheese is melted, stirring frequently.

In a large shallow casserole spread noodles, arrange turkey on top, sprinkle over chopped broccoli stems, lay in gently broccoli flowerets, gently pour cream sauce over all, and strew almonds on top. Bake in moderate oven, 350°, 15 minutes, or until bubbling. Serves 4–6, depending upon amount of turkey and broccoli.

TURKEY HASH

2 cups LO turkey chopped   ¼ cup chopped ripe olives
    or diced   4 tablespoons turkey or
2 tablespoons butter or   chicken broth
    margarine   ¾ cup cream
2 tablespoons minced onion   2 egg yolks
1 tablespoon chopped green   salt and pepper
    pepper

The name hash here is misnomer, because the dish is more
of a creamed turkey; but it is quite widely known as hash.

Melt butter in skillet and sauté onion and green pepper
until onion shows a little color. Stir in turkey, olives, and
broth and simmer until turkey is thoroughly heated. Blend
egg yolks with cream and stir in, stirring constantly until
somewhat thickened. Season to taste. Serve in pastry shells
or toasted bread cases (see under recipe for Chicken Patties, p. 95).   SERVES 4–5.

TURKEY CUTLETS

2 cups LO turkey meat   ½ cup minced mushrooms
    chopped or diced fine   sautéed
1 cup thick cream sauce   flour
3 eggs   fine bread crumbs
                                  fat

Make the cream sauce with 3 tablespoons butter or margarine, 3 tablespoons flour, and 1 cup milk. Stir constantly
until thick and smooth and season to taste. Beat 2 eggs
lightly, stir in a little of the hot cream sauce, and then blend
the eggs quickly into the sauce. Add turkey meat and

mushrooms and cook until well blended and hot, stirring constantly. Spread on a buttered platter and chill.

When the mixture is cold, form into small cutlets by rolling between the palms or patting into shape. Roll the cutlets in flour, then in the third egg lightly beaten with a fork and a teaspoon or so of water, and finally in the bread crumbs. Let stand at least 15–20 minutes to dry the coating, or chill in the refrigerator. Sauté in butter or margarine or bacon fat until golden brown all over, or fry in deep fat (390°) and drain on brown paper or paper towels. Serve with tomato sauce, mushroom sauce, or LO turkey gravy.   SERVES 4.

TURKEY LOAF

2 generous cups LO turkey diced small

4 tablespoons butter or margarine

6 tablespoons flour

2 cups milk

1 cup turkey broth or chicken consommé

salt and pepper

1 teaspoon minced parsley

3 tablespoons minced pimiento

½ cup fine bread crumbs

¼ cup minced celery

3 eggs well beaten

Melt butter in large skillet, blend in flour, cook for 2–3 minutes, and blend in milk and turkey broth. Stir constantly until sauce is smooth and thick. Season to taste and mix in parsley, pimiento, bread crumbs, celery, and turkey. Remove from heat and stir in eggs. Turn into large well-greased loaf pan or mold and bake in moderate oven, 350°, about 35 minutes, or until center is firm to the touch. Let stand 2–3 minutes, run a spatula around the sides, and unmold on heated platter. Serve with leftover turkey gravy, rich cream sauce, or mushroom sauce.   SERVES 6.

TURKEY PIE

3–4 *cups LO turkey diced*
2 *cups turkey broth*
1 *medium onion sliced*
2 *carrots sliced*
½ *cup celery chopped*
1 *clove garlic*
2 *cloves*
½ *cup flour*

½ *cup butter*
2 *cups light cream or*
    evaporated milk
dash of nutmeg
1 *teaspoon lemon juice*
salt and pepper
pastry crust

To get the necessary broth for this dish cook turkey carcass as you would for soup. Put in a kettle the broth, onion, carrots, celery, garlic clove stuck on a toothpick, and cloves. Bring to boil and simmer 15–20 minutes, or until vegetables are tender. Remove garlic, thicken with flour and butter kneaded together, and blend in cream. Add nutmeg, lemon juice, and turkey, and taste for seasoning. Pour in a casserole that just holds it and cover with your favorite pastry, rolled thin and slashed several times to let the steam escape. Bake at 400° for 10 minutes, lower heat to 350°, and bake 10 minutes longer, or until crust is brown. Glaze before baking—that is, brush with ice water, milk or cream, or melted shortening. SERVES 6–8.

TURKEY TERRAPIN

3 cups LO turkey diced

3 tablespoons butter or
margarine

2 tablespoons flour

1½ cups turkey broth or
gravy thinned with
broth or dry white wine

3 tomatoes skinned and
chopped

1 teaspoon tomato paste

2 tablespoons minced onion

¾ cup sliced and sautéed
mushrooms

1 tablespoon chives cut fine

1 tablespoon minced
parsley

¼ teaspoon nutmeg

2 tablespoons brandy

2 tablespoons sherry

Melt butter in heavy skillet, blend in flour until smooth,
and gradually add broth, stirring constantly until thickened.
Add tomatoes, tomato paste, onion, mushrooms, chives,
parsley, and nutmeg. Simmer about 5 minutes. Check seasoning. Stir in turkey, brandy, and sherry. Cover, and simmer over lowest possible heat until piping hot. Serve at
once. Serve over hot fluffy rice, buttered noodles, or, best
of all, fresh hot cornbread split and generously buttered.

SERVES 6–7.

TURKEY RAGOUT

2–3 *cups LO turkey cut in 1-inch wide strips*
2 *tablespoons butter or margarine*
2 *tablespoons chopped onion*
1 *tablespoon browned flour (2 tablespoons if broth is used instead of gravy)*
½ *teaspoon Worcestershire sauce*

pinch of nutmeg
1–1½ *cups LO turkey gravy slightly thinned or turkey or chicken broth*
salt and pepper
½ *cup chopped stuffed olives*
1–2 *tablespoons cranberry or currant jelly*
¼–⅓ *cup sherry or Madeira*

Melt butter in skillet, sauté onion lightly, blend in browned flour, and stir in gravy or broth. When sauce is smooth and thickened add Worcestershire sauce, nutmeg, salt and pepper to taste, and olives. When well blended add turkey strips, stir gently to be sure they are well coated, cover, and simmer over lowest possible heat 8–10 minutes. Stir in jelly and wine, and heat until jelly is dissolved, stirring constantly but gently. Serve on fresh buttered toast, waffles, buttered noodles, or hot cornbread split and buttered.

SERVES 4–6.

TURKEY-SPAGHETTI CASSEROLE

2 cups LO turkey diced
¼ pound spaghetti broken
   in 2-inch lengths
¼ cup diced pimiento
¼ cup chopped green
   pepper
¼ cup chopped onion

1 can cream of mushroom
   soup undiluted
½ cup turkey broth or
   diluted gravy
1½ cups grated sharp cheese
salt and pepper

Cook spaghetti to the degree of softness you want it—8–10 minutes in rapidly boiling salted water cooks it *al dente*, or with a touch of chewiness still left. Drain, rinse in cold water, and drain again. In a large bowl mix spaghetti, turkey, pimiento, green pepper, onion, cream of mushroom soup, turkey broth, and all but ½ cup of the cheese. Stir all this lightly but until it is thoroughly mixed. Pour in 6-cup casserole, top with remaining cheese, and bake 35–45 minutes in moderate oven, 350°. (If you have made the casserole ahead of time and stored it in the refrigerator, let it come to room temperature before baking, or bake an additional 10 minutes.)   SERVES 4–5.

Combine vinegar, water, salt, and sugar, pour over cut-up turkey, stir thoroughly, and let marinate in a cool place or in the refrigerator 2–3 hours. Add celery and grapes, and toss lightly but well with mayonnaise. Arrange on crisp lettuce leaves and garnish bowl with olives (black or stuffed) and sliced hard-cooked eggs. SERVES 5–6.

FISH

FISH

FISH CHOWDER

2 cups any LO white fish
    coarsely flaked
⅛ pound fat salt pork diced
    fine or 4 strips bacon
    chopped
1 cup chopped onion
2 cups potato peeled and
    diced small

1 cup water
1 can condensed cream of
    celery soup
1 can condensed clam
    chowder
2½ cups milk
salt and pepper
3 tablespoons minced
    parsley

This chowder is quite different from the conventional New England Fish Chowder, which is always made with raw fish, but it makes a fine hearty meal any time you have a fair quantity of boiled or baked white fish left over.

In a good-sized soup kettle brown salt pork or bacon until crisp. Skim out the pieces and reserve. In the fat cook onion until soft but not colored. Turn in potatoes and stir in the fat a minute or two. Add water, both soups, and milk, stirring until well blended. Season to taste, gently stir in flaked fish, salt pork or bacon bits, and 2 tablespoons of the parsley, and heat until piping hot. Turn into large soup plates or a soup tureen and sprinkle remaining parsley on top.   SERVES 8.

CREAMED FISH IN SCALLOP SHELLS

3 cups LO cooked fish or
    shellfish
¼ cup dry white wine, fish
    bouillon, or chicken
    broth
2 tablespoons minced
    mushrooms

1 tablespoon butter or
    margarine
1½ cups thick cream sauce
grated Parmesan cheese
melted butter

Skin and bone fish, but leave in as large pieces as possible.
Lay in skillet, with wine, mushrooms, and butter. Cover
and cook over low heat just long enough to heat through.

Make cream sauce with 3 tablespoons butter or margarine, 3 tablespoons flour, and 1½ cups milk. Cook until
smooth and thick, season to taste, and carefully strain liquid
from fish into it to thin it some.

Gently break fish into uniform pieces, rather small. Put 2
tablespoons sauce in center of each of 6 large scallop shells
(or shallow casserole) and spread out. Divide fish among
the shells and cover with remaining sauce. Sprinkle tops
with grated cheese, dribble a little butter over each, and
brown quickly in 450° oven or under broiler.   SERVES 6.

DEVILED FISH IN SCALLOP SHELLS

3 cups LO cooked fish or
    shellfish
3 tablespoons butter or
    margarine
2 tablespoons minced onion
2 tablespoons water
2 cups cream sauce

1½ teaspoons prepared
    mustard
2 egg yolks beaten lightly
2 tablespoons whipped
    cream
2 tablespoons grated
    Parmesan cheese

Heat 1 tablespoon of the butter in skillet and sauté onion
lightly. Add fish, skinned, boned, and broken into quite

small pieces but not flaked. Add water, cover, and cook over low heat until water is cooked away.

Prepare cream sauce with 3 tablespoons butter or margarine, 3 tablespoons flour, and 2 cups milk, cooking until smooth, and seasoning to taste. In another saucepan melt remaining 2 tablespoons of butter, blend in mustard, and stir in 1½ cups of the cream sauce. Stir in egg yolks quickly, add fish, and correct seasoning. Fill scallop shells with mixture, or use a shallow casserole. Fold whipped cream into remaining ½ cup of cream sauce and spread over top of shells or casserole. Sprinkle with cheese and brown quickly in hot oven, 450°, or under broiler.   SERVES 6.

FISH AU GRATIN

2 cups LO cooked fish
2 tablespoons water
1 tablespoon butter or margarine
2 cups cream sauce
2 cups hot fluffy mashed potatoes

4 tablespoons grated cheese (Gruyère, Cheddar, or American)
grated Parmesan cheese
melted butter

To reheat cooked fish, break carefully into fairly large pieces, removing skin and bones. Heat water and butter in skillet, lay in pieces of fish gently, cover loosely (leave vent for evaporation), and heat over low heat just until water has evaporated.

Make cream sauce with 3 tablespoons butter or margarine, 3 tablespoons flour, and 2 cups milk. Cook until smooth, stirring constantly, season to taste, and blend in the 4 tablespoons cheese. Arrange mashed potatoes around edge of shallow well-greased casserole, using pastry bag if possible. Spread half of the cream sauce in the center of the casserole, lay in pieces of fish, and cover with remaining sauce. (Do not cover potatoes.) Sprinkle top of sauce with Parmesan cheese, brush top of potatoes with melted butter, and brown in hot oven, 450°, or under broiler.

SERVES 4.

FISH CAKES

1½ cups LO cooked white
    fish flaked
1½ cups LO mashed
    potatoes
3 tablespoons thin cream or
    top milk

½ teaspoon salt
dash of pepper
3 tablespoons bacon fat,
    butter, or margarine

Mix fish, potatoes, and cream thoroughly, add salt if needed
(it is likely not to be necessary) and pepper, and shape in
flat cakes ½–¾ inch thick. Flour your hands if potato-fish
mixture tends to stick. Heat fat to sizzling in heavy skillet,
lay in cakes, turn heat to low, and brown to good deep
color on both sides. Serve with tomato sauce (canned will
do). Or shape in balls the size of a small egg, chill, and
fry in deep fat (390°) to a golden brown. Drain on brown
paper or paper toweling.   SERVES 5–6.

Caution: If fat is not hot enough fish balls will break up
in small pieces.

FISH OR SHRIMP CREOLE

2 cups LO cooked fish or
    shrimp broken in small
    pieces
¼ cup butter or margarine
2 tablespoons chopped
    onion
⅔ cup chopped celery
2 tablespoons chopped
    green pepper

4 tablespoons flour
2½ cups canned tomatoes
⅓ cup water
1 small bay leaf
½ teaspoon chopped parsley
¼ teaspoon chervil

Leftover fish or shrimp prepared in this manner provides a
fine hearty meal of excellent flavor.

    Melt butter in skillet and cook onion, celery, and green

pepper about 5 minutes over low heat, stirring frequently. Blend in flour, cook until smooth and slightly browned, and stir in tomatoes and water. Cook, stirring constantly, until it is somewhat thickened. Add bay leaf, parsley, chervil, and fish or shrimp, stir well, cover, lower heat, and simmer 12–15 minutes. Serve over hot fluffy rice.   SERVES 6.

FISH PIE

2 cups LO fish broken in medium chunks (almost any fish will do, especially any white-fleshed fish)

2½ tablespoons butter or margarine

2 medium onions sliced

2 hard-cooked eggs sliced

2 small tomatoes peeled and sliced (opt.)

salt and pepper

2 cups fresh mashed potatoes

1 raw egg well beaten

This is an easy dish and a very good one. Put ½ tablespoon of the butter in a casserole and melt it. Heat 1 tablespoon butter in skillet and lightly brown onions. Stir in fish and mix gently, just enough to coat fish. Arrange in casserole, and lay in slices of egg and tomato among the fish pieces. (This is easy if you put in a spoonful of fish and then egg and tomato slices against it, repeating until casserole is filled.) Salt and pepper to taste. Mix about ¾ of the beaten egg with the mashed potatoes and spread over top of casserole. Dot with remaining butter and brush with beaten egg. Bake about 25 minutes in moderate oven, 400°, or until top is well browned.   SERVES 5–6.

FISH PINWHEELS

1 cup LO white fish of any kind, or part salmon, shrimp, crab, or lobster flaked coarsely

2 tablespoons butter or margarine

2 tablespoons chopped onion

2 tablespoons flour

¾ cup milk

1 tablespoon minced parsley

¼ cup diced celery

salt and pepper

1 recipe biscuits

Melt butter in skillet and lightly brown onion. Stir in flour, cook a moment, and gradually add milk, stirring constantly until sauce is thick and smooth. Remove from heat and add parsley, celery, flaked fish, and salt and pepper to taste. Roll out or pat your favorite biscuit dough on floured waxed paper, shaping it into a rectangle a little less than ½ inch thick. Spread fish mixture over dough and roll up the long way like a jelly roll. By lifting the waxed paper as you roll you can handle the soft dough without breaking it up. With a well-greased sharp knife cut the roll in 1-inch slices, laying each in a large greased pie plate as it is cut. Bake in a hot oven, 425°, 12–15 minutes, or until well browned. Serve with cheese sauce, made by adding 1 cup grated cheese to 2 cups rich cream sauce.   SERVES 5–6.

FISH SOUFFLÉ

2 cups LO white fish flaked
   —cod, haddock, floun-
   der, or similar fish, or
   canned fish flakes
2 cups medium cream
   sauce

4 eggs separated
1 additional egg white
2 tablespoons buttered
   crumbs
1 tablespoon grated
   Parmesan cheese

This is a simple but pleasant dish. If you don't have quite
enough leftover fish for it, add a can of lobster, crabmeat,
or shrimp.

Make cream sauce of 3 tablespoons butter, 3 tablespoons
flour, and 2 cups light cream or top milk. Season to taste.
Remove from fire and stir in egg yolks well beaten. Add
flaked fish. Cool to lukewarm and fold in egg whites beaten
until stiff. Pour into greased 6-cup casserole, top with buttered crumbs mixed with cheese, and bake in 350° oven
about 30 minutes, or until knife inserted in center comes
out clean.   SERVES 5–6.

FISH-STUFFED EGGS (Hot or Cold)

¼ cup LO fish, flaked fine
6 hard-cooked eggs
1 teaspoon prepared
   mustard

2 teaspoons soft butter
dash cayenne pepper
½ teaspoon curry powder
mayonnaise

Slit eggs lengthwise and remove yolks to a bowl. Rub them
through a fine sieve, or mash thoroughly. Mix with fish,
mustard, butter, cayenne, and curry powder. Blend with
just enough mayonnaise to hold it together. Stuff egg whites
with this mixture and chill.

If you prefer to make these eggs into a hot dish, omit
butter in preparing them. Lay stuffed eggs in a shallow
greased casserole and cover with a cup of rich cream

sauce, made with 2 tablespoons butter, 2 tablespoons flour, and 1 cup top milk or half cream, half milk. Season to taste. This sauce is improved by the addition of ¼ cup (generous) sharp grated cheese and the lightly beaten yolk of an egg. Or make 1½ cups of cream sauce and blend in a small tin of crabmeat or lobster coarsely flaked. Bake the casserole 15 minutes in a moderate oven, 375°, or until lightly browned.   SERVES 6.

FISH WITH SOUR CREAM

2 cups LO cooked fish
    broken in large chunks
2 tablespoons butter or
    margarine
1 small onion minced

1 teaspoon paprika
1 cup sour cream
2 egg yolks lightly beaten
1 tablespoon lemon juice
salt and pepper

Sour cream addicts will find this a very simple and most delicious way to use almost any leftover fish, though it is best with a fairly solid white fish.

Melt butter and lightly brown onion. Stir in paprika (don't skimp on it). Add sour cream and heat almost to boiling, stirring constantly. Stir a little of the cream into the egg yolks and add to remaining cream. Cook over low heat, stirring gently, until slightly thickened. Add fish and reheat, but do not let sauce boil. Stir in lemon juice and serve immediately, over hot fluffy rice.   SERVES 4.

FISH AND VEGETABLE CASSEROLE

2 *cups LO fish, flaked*
2 *tablespoons sherry (opt.)*
4 *tablespoons butter*
1 *medium onion minced*
4 *tablespoons flour*
1 *can condensed chicken broth (or 3 chicken bouillon cubes to 1 cup boiling water)*
1 *cup milk*

salt
paprika
1 *cup cooked diced celery*
1 *cup cooked green peas*
1 *cup cooked diced carrots*
2 *tablespoons bread crumbs*
2 *tablespoons grated American or Parmesan cheese*

Pour sherry over fish and let stand while you prepare other ingredients. Melt butter in large skillet and sauté onion until soft but not brown. Blend in flour and stir in chicken broth and milk until sauce is thick and smooth. Add salt and paprika to taste. Stir in vegetables and fish and pour in large greased casserole. Top with mixed crumbs and cheese (and a little more butter if you feel generous) and bake at 375° until brown, about ½ hour.   SERVES 6.

KEDGEREE I

1 *cup LO cooked fish, white fish or salmon, flaked*
1 *cup LO boiled rice*
1 *scant tablespoon butter or margarine*
2 *tablespoons minced onion*
1 *hard-cooked egg chopped*

1 *tablespoon minced parsley*
2 *tablespoons curry powder*
½ *teaspoon Worcestershire sauce*
2 *tablespoons sherry*

This curry-flavored fish and rice dish, like many widely known classics, is made in many ways. This one is simple, quick, and good.

Melt butter in skillet, and sauté the onion in it until it is yellow. Stir in rice, egg, parsley, curry powder, and Worcestershire sauce. Mix well and cook a minute or two. Lightly stir in flaked fish and sherry, and turn into well-greased casserole. Cover and bake 10 minutes in 400° oven. Serve with quarters of hard-cooked eggs as a garnish. SERVES 4.

KEDGEREE II

2 cups LO cooked fish, such as salmon or halibut, broken in pieces but not flaked (or part cooked shrimp, lobster, or crab-meat)

2 tablespoons bacon fat, olive oil, or butter

3 tablespoons minced onion

1 cup dry raw rice

2 cups chicken broth or water

salt to taste

3 cups cream sauce

1 tablespoon curry powder

2 hard-cooked eggs chopped

1 hard-cooked egg yolk pressed through sieve

1 teaspoon minced parsley

This kedgeree is a more elaborate dish than the preceding one, a good dish for company.

Heat bacon fat in heavy skillet, cook onion lightly, stir in rice, and cook over low heat until rice is yellow, stirring frequently. Add broth, cover tightly, and cook over low heat until liquid is absorbed and rice tender. Salt to taste.

While rice is cooking make cream sauce with 4 table-spoons butter or margarine, 4 tablespoons flour, and 3 cups milk. Stir until smooth and season to taste. Blend in curry powder. Stir in fish and chopped egg, and leave over low heat until hot, stirring frequently.

Put half the rice mixture in a serving casserole, pour over half the fish mixture, add remaining rice and remaining fish. Sprinkle top with sieved egg yolk mixed with parsley.   SERVES 4–5.

HADDOCK HASH

1 *cup LO haddock flaked*   *salt and pepper*
    coarsely   *dash cayenne pepper*
1 *cup chopped LO boiled*   *pinch nutmeg*
    potatoes   1 *tablespoon bacon fat*

Mix flaked haddock and potatoes lightly, add seasoning to taste. Heat fat in heavy skillet and turn in mixture. Brown lightly over medium heat, stir with a fork, add a little more fat if necessary, and brown well on the bottom. Fold over like an omelet and slide on heated platter. Garnish with tomato slices browned in bacon fat or tomato halves broiled.

SERVES 3.

SALMON SALAD SANDWICHES

1 *cup LO cooked salmon*   1 *tablespoon French*
    flaked   *dressing*
¼ *cup chopped celery*   1 *tablespoon mayonnaise*
¼ *cup chopped green*   *salt*
    pepper   *buttered bread*
¼ *cup crisp lettuce shredded*

Mix salmon, celery, green pepper, and lettuce. Bind with French dressing and mayonnaise or use 2 tablespoons mayonnaise. Season to taste and spread on slices of white, whole wheat, or pumpernickel bread. Top with second slices, press rather firmly, trim crusts, and cut in halves, thirds, or quarters. Makes enough to spread about 8–9 slices.

Note: This mixture is also good as stuffing for small finger rolls.

SWORDFISH "REPRISE"

4 good-sized serving pieces
   of LO broiled swordfish
¾ cup dry white wine
¼ cup water
1 tablespoon minced
   parsley
1 teaspoon chopped chives
2 tablespoons chopped
   celery

2 tablespoons butter or
   margarine
4 shallots or scallions (little
   green onions) chopped
½ cup sliced mushrooms
1 tablespoon flour
1 egg yolk
¼ cup heavy cream
salt and pepper

This recipe is less trouble than it looks, and it makes leftover swordfish into a dish that some people think is better
than broiled fresh swordfish.

Put in a skillet the wine, water, parsley, chives, celery,
and 1 tablespoon of the butter. Lay in the pieces of swordfish gently with a spatula, cover, and heat just to the boiling point. While it is heating melt the remaining butter in
another skillet and sauté shallots (or scallions) and mushrooms until shallots begin to show color. Sift flour over,
blend well, cook for a moment, and strain liquid from fish
into mixture. Cook until smooth and somewhat thickened.
Blend egg yolk and cream well and quickly stir into sauce.
Heat well but not to the boiling point. Lift pieces of fish
onto hot serving dish and pour sauce over.   SERVES 4.

SAVORY SWORDFISH

2–3 cups LO broiled sword-
    fish cut in 1-inch cubes
¼ cup olive oil or cooking
    oil
2 onions chopped
2 stalks celery chopped
2 young carrots chopped

1 clove garlic mashed
1 tablespoon capers
1 whole clove
1 small bay leaf
salt and pepper
1 cup dry white wine

This is another way of making the most of leftover swordfish. Both dishes are good enough to warrant your being
generous in your original purchase of swordfish, just to be
sure to have another meal from it.

    Heat oil in heavy skillet and cook chopped vegetables
and garlic until slightly colored. Add capers, clove, bay
leaf, salt and pepper to taste, and wine. Cover and simmer
over very low heat about 5 minutes. Lay in pieces of swordfish, stir carefully, cover again, and simmer until swordfish
is piping hot. Serve on hot fluffy rice or buttered noodles.

SERVES 5–6.

TUNA STUFFED GREEN PEPPERS

2½ cups LO boiled rice
6 medium green peppers
6½-ounce can tuna fish
2 tablespoons grated onion

½ cup grated sharp cheese
¾ cup milk
salt and pepper
dash Tabasco sauce

When you are cooking rice cook enough to have it on hand
for this flavorsome dish.

    Carefully cut tops off green peppers, clean out seeds and
membranes, and parboil in boiling salted water 4–5 minutes, or until partially tender but still crisp. Turn upside
down and drain. Shred tuna coarsely and mix lightly with
rice, onion, cheese, milk, salt and pepper to taste, and

Tabasco sauce. Fill pepper shells and place in shallow greased casserole which just holds them. Add ¼ cup of water to the casserole and bake in moderate oven, 350°, 30 minutes. Serve with tomato sauce.   SERVES 6.

SHELLFISH

SHELLFISH

SEAFOOD BISQUE

1 cup LO cooked shrimp,
    crabmeat, lobster, or
    mixture of these
    chopped very fine
2 tablespoons butter or
    margarine
1 teaspoon minced onion
2 tablespoons flour

2½ cups top milk or 1½ cups
    chicken broth and 1
    cup light cream
salt and pepper
dash cayenne pepper or
    Tabasco sauce
1 teaspoon minced parsley

Melt butter in skillet, cook onion gently until soft but not colored, stir in flour and cook a moment. Slowly add milk or chicken broth and cream, minced seafood, and seasoning to taste. Turn into large double boiler and heat over boiling water 15–20 minutes. Pour into soup plates or large tureen and sprinkle with parsley.   SERVES 4.

Note: If you have an electric blender you can produce a velvety smooth bisque by putting seafood and liquid in the blender 10–15 seconds before adding to the butter-flour *roux.*

SEAFOOD CASSEROLE

2 *cups LO shrimp*	*salt and pepper*
1 *cup LO crabmeat*	½ *teaspoon minced parsley*
1 *pint shelled oysters*	1 *small can pimiento*
3 *tablespoons butter*	*chopped*
½ *pound sliced mushrooms*	2 *tablespoons sherry (opt.)*
1 *green pepper chopped*	3 *tablespoons bread crumbs*
2 *cups rich cream sauce*	

Heat oysters in their own liquor until edges curl. Drain.
Melt 2 tablespoons butter in skillet and cook mushrooms
and green pepper 4–5 minutes over medium heat. Make
cream sauce with 3 tablespoons butter, 3 tablespoons
flour, and 2 cups light cream or 1 cup light cream and 1
cup dry white wine. Season to taste and simmer a few minutes. Stir in cooked mushrooms and pepper, parsley, pimiento, sherry, and seafood. Pour in greased 2-quart casserole, top with crumbs, dot with remaining tablespoon of
butter, and bake at 375° for 20–30 minutes, or until thoroughly heated and well browned.   SERVES 6–8.

SEAFOOD CASSEROLE WITH DEVILED EGGS

1 *cup LO seafood (shrimp,*	1½ *cups medium cream*
salmon, tuna, crab-	*sauce*
meat, or lobster, or any	½ *cup grated sharp cheese*
combination of these)	1 *cup sliced mushrooms*
6 *hard-cooked eggs*	*sautéed or 1 small can*
2 *tablespoons mayonnaise*	¾ *cup cooked green peas*
¼ *teaspoon dry mustard*	*(opt.)*
salt and pepper	

Shell eggs, cut in half lengthwise, and remove yolks to a
bowl. Mash until smooth or force through fine sieve, and
blend with mayonnaise, mustard, salt and pepper to taste.
Stuff egg whites with this mixture and arrange in shallow

casserole. Make cream sauce with 2 tablespoons butter or
margarine, 2 tablespoons flour, and 1½ cups whole milk.
Season to taste, add cheese, and cook until cheese is melted,
stirring constantly. Add mushrooms, peas, and seafood, mix
well, and pour gently around eggs in casserole. Spoon a bit
of sauce over the top of each egg. Bake 25 minutes in moderate oven, 375°.   SERVES 6.

SEAFOOD SHEPHERD'S PIE

2–3 cups LO white fish,
  shrimp, scallops, crab-
  meat, lobster, or any
  combination
1 cup LO carrots diced or
  sliced
1 cup sliced onions sautéed
1 cup LO green peas
2 cups cream sauce

2 tablespoons lemon juice
½ teaspoon Worcestershire
  sauce
salt and pepper
2–3 cups hot mashed
  potatoes
1 tablespoon butter
2 tablespoons grated cheese

This is a versatile dish, since it can make use of almost any
combination of leftover white fish of any kind, and almost
any seafoods; the vegetables can be altered, too. String
beans cut up, cauliflower flowerets, braised celery, or asparagus can be used.

Arrange fish, well mixed, and mixed vegetables in layers
in a greased casserole. Make cream sauce with 3 tablespoons butter or margarine, 3 tablespoons flour, and 2 cups
milk. Add to it the lemon juice, Worcestershire, and salt
and pepper to taste. Pour over casserole. Spread well-
whipped mashed potato over the top, either as a smooth
topping or arranged around the edge, leaving the center
uncovered. Top potato with dots of butter and sprinkle with
cheese. Bake in hot oven, 400°, 25–30 minutes, or until
sauce is bubbling and potatoes are golden brown.

SERVES 6–8.

SEAFOOD PIE

2 cups LO fish and shellfish ½ cup cooked green pepper
    (crab, lobster, shrimp,   chopped
    or any combination) 2 teaspoons finely minced
⅓ cup tomato catsup   onion
⅓ cup chili sauce salt and pepper
½ cup cooked celery ½ recipe pastry
    chopped 1 cup cheese sauce

Roll out your favorite pastry ⅛ inch thick and line pie plate.
Prick the bottom well, cover with a circle of waxed paper,
and cover it with raw rice or dried beans or peas to weight
the crust down. Bake 10 minutes in hot oven, 450°, remove from oven, shake out rice, and remove waxed paper.
Mix seafood, catsup, chili sauce, green pepper, celery, onion, and salt and pepper to taste. Pour into partially cooked
shell. Make cheese sauce with 2 tablespoons butter or margarine, 2 tablespoons flour, and ¾ cup milk. Season to taste
and stir in 1 cup loosely packed, grated sharp cheese. Pour
cheese sauce on top of casserole and bake about 25 minutes in moderate oven, 400°.   SERVES 6.

SEAFOOD CROQUETTES

2 cups minced LO fish, dash of cayenne pepper
    crab, lobster, or shrimp, 2 eggs
    or mixture 2 tablespoons heavy cream
1 cup thick cream sauce 2 tablespoons sherry
1 teaspoon minced parsley fine bread crumbs
1 teaspoon minced onion fat for deep frying
salt to taste

Make cream sauce with 3 tablespoons butter or margarine,
3 tablespoons flour, and 1 cup rich milk. When it is smooth
and thick stir in seafood, parsley, onion, salt to taste, and
cayenne. Simmer over very low heat 8–10 minutes, stirring

frequently. Beat 1 egg with heavy cream and stir in. Cook a moment, remove from stove, and add sherry. Spread on a cold platter and chill. Shape into croquettes (flour your hands if mixture sticks), cone-shaped, pear-shaped, or sausage-shaped. Roll in crumbs, dip in egg beaten lightly with 1 tablespoon of water, and roll again in crumbs. Chill. Fry in deep fat (390°) a few at a time. Drain well. Serve with tomato sauce.   SERVES 4–5.

SEAFOOD-WILD RICE CASSEROLE

3 cups LO shrimp, lobster, or crabmeat, or 1 cup each
1 cup wild rice
2 tablespoons butter
2 medium onions sliced thin
1 green pepper chopped
¼ teaspoon thyme
½ teaspoon marjoram

6 tablespoons chili sauce or tomato catsup or ½ cup condensed tomato soup and 1 tablespoon tomato paste
½ cup light cream
salt
paprika

Wild rice makes a party dish out of almost anything, and is a perfect base for this dish. For ordinary occasions plain rice will do, but use converted rice, which never gets gummy or gluey, and cook according to directions on the package.

Cook wild rice in 3 quarts boiling salted water until tender, about 25–30 minutes. Drain but do not rinse. Put in bottom of greased 2-quart casserole. Melt butter in skillet and cook onion and green pepper until soft but not browned. Arrange over rice. Mix seafood and arrange as next layer in casserole. Sprinkle with herbs. Mix chili sauce or soup and cream and pour over all. Season with a light sprinkling of salt and paprika and bake in 375° oven about 20 minutes or until thoroughly heated.   SERVES 6.

CRAB CANAPÉ LORENZO

1 *cup LO crabmeat flaked*
2 *tablespoons butter or margarine*
1 *teaspoon minced shallot or onion*
½ *teaspoon paprika*
¼ *teaspoon dry mustard*
¼ *teaspoon salt*
2 *tablespoons flour*
½ *cup light cream*
1 *teaspoon Worcestershire sauce*
small rounds of bread toasted on one side
2 *tablespoons grated Parmesan cheese*
1 *tablespoon milk*

This is one of the most delicious of hot hors d'oeuvres, and is quite practical because the mixture can be made hours ahead and merely browned at the last minute.

Heat butter in skillet and cook shallot until soft but not colored. Add crabmeat and sauté a moment. Stir in paprika, mustard, salt, and flour. Cook a moment and blend in cream and Worcestershire sauce. Just before serving time spread quite thickly on untoasted side of bread rounds. Mix cheese and milk and use as topping for crab mixture. Bake in a hot oven, 400°, 10–15 minutes, or until lightly browned, or brown under broiler, placing at least 2 inches below flame.

CRABMEAT AND CORN CHOWDER

2½ *cups LO corn cut from the cob*
1 *cup cooked crabmeat flaked*
1 *tablespoon minced onion*
2½ *cups scalded milk*
2½ *cups thin cream sauce*
2 *egg yolks*
salt and pepper
dash of nutmeg
1 *tablespoon butter*

Score the ears of corn before you cut the kernels off, and after cutting off the corn run the back of the knife down the cob to get out all of the milk. Put in top of double boiler the corn, onion, and hot milk, and cook over boiling water 20–25 minutes. Then force the mixture through a coarse sieve or food mill, or, if you have an electric blender give it 30 seconds to 1 minute in the blender. Put in kettle with cream sauce (made with 3 tablespoons butter or margarine, 3 tablespoons flour, and 2½ cups whole milk) and bring slowly to boil. Beat in egg yolks vigorously, one at a time, season to taste, add nutmeg, and just before serving stir in crabmeat and butter.   SERVES 8.

CRABMEAT SANDWICHES

1 cup LO cooked crabmeat flaked
¼ cup celery chopped fine
1 hard-cooked egg chopped
salt and pepper
½ teaspoon minced parsley
2 tablespoons mayonnaise
dash paprika
buttered bread

Mix ingredients thoroughly and spread fairly generously on white or whole wheat bread, thinly sliced, crusts removed. Add top slices and press together. Will cover about 6 slices, which can be cut into halves, thirds, or quarters.

Note: This mixture is also good as stuffing for small finger rolls.

QUICK CRAB ASPIC

1 cup LO crabmeat
1 can prepared aspic
1 teaspoon lemon juice
1 teaspoon grated onion
1 cup finely chopped celery

Melt the canned aspic over boiling water in a double boiler. Mix with crabmeat, lemon juice, onion, and celery. Check seasoning and add a little salt if needed. Pour in ring mold which has been rinsed out in cold water and chill until set. Unmold on chilled platter and fill center with mixed vegetable salad.   SERVES 6.

CRABMEAT CAKES

1 *cup LO crabmeat flaked*   *pinch of thyme*
½ *cup soft bread crumbs*   *salt and pepper to taste*
1 *egg (unbeaten)*   *flour*
½ *teaspoon dry mustard*   *fat for deep frying*

Blend well crabmeat, bread crumbs, egg, mustard, thyme, and salt and pepper to taste. Form into small cakes, roll in flour, and chill. When ready to serve, fry to golden brown in deep fat heated to 375°. Drain on brown paper or paper toweling. Serve with Newburg Sauce. (Make this sauce by stirring 2 egg yolks into 1 cup rich cream sauce, and cooking a few minutes over hot water. Add 2 tablespoons dry sherry.)   SERVES 3.

CRABMEAT COLESLAW

1 *cup LO crabmeat*   ½ *cup chopped celery*
2 *cups shredded cabbage*   *salt*
1 *small apple chopped (do*   2 *tablespoons chili sauce*
     not peel)   ½ *cup mayonnaise*

Crabmeat and apple make this an unusual coleslaw. Shred cabbage very fine and soak 20–30 minutes in ice water to crisp. Drain well and dry in a towel. Blend with apple, celery and crabmeat and salt to taste. Mix chili sauce with mayonnaise and stir into mixture.   SERVES 4–5.

CRAB SOUFFLÉ

1 cup LO crabmeat flaked
1 cup cream sauce
1 teaspoon Worcestershire
    sauce

½ teaspoon minced parsley
3 eggs separated
2 tablespoons buttered
    crumbs

Make the cream sauce with 2½ tablespoons butter, 2½ tablespoons flour, and 1 cup top milk or light cream. Season to taste, add Worcestershire sauce, parsley, and yolks of eggs well beaten. Cool and fold in stiffly beaten egg whites. Top with crumbs and bake in 350° oven about 35 minutes, or until knife inserted in center comes out clean.

SERVES 4.

CRABMEAT-STUFFED AVOCADO

LO cooked crabmeat
avocado halves chilled
lemon juice
hard-cooked egg

chopped parsley or chives
French dressing or
    mayonnaise

Fill cavities of avocado halves loosely with crabmeat—do not pack. Sprinkle crabmeat and cut surface of avocados with lemon juice, about 1 teaspoon to a serving, and cover the whole with hard-cooked egg chopped and forced through a coarse sieve. (1 large egg will serve for 4 avocado halves.) Sprinkle with parsley or chives and serve at once with either French dressing or mayonnaise.

CREAMED CRAB AND MUSHROOMS

¾ cup LO crabmeat flaked
½ pound mushrooms sliced
3 tablespoons butter
1 teaspoon chopped chives
2 teaspoons chopped
    shallots (or onion)

1 teaspoon minced parsley
2 tablespoons flour
1½ cups sour cream
salt and pepper
dash of nutmeg
2 tablespoons sherry

Put mushrooms in a saucepan, barely cover with water, and cook 10 minutes over low heat. Drain, but reserve liquid. Melt butter in skillet and sauté lightly chives, shallots or onion, and parsley. Blend in flour smoothly and cook a moment. Add mushroom liquid to sour cream, mix well, and add to skillet. Cook until smooth and thickened, stirring constantly. Season to taste with salt and pepper, add nutmeg, and stir in crabmeat. Cover and cook over lowest possible heat 5 minutes. Stir in sherry and serve at once over fresh unbuttered toast.   SERVES 5–6.

DEVILED CRAB

1 cup LO cooked crabmeat
    flaked
½ cup soft bread crumbs
½ cup cream sauce
1 tablespoon minced green
    pepper
1 tablespoon minced onion
1 tablespoon chopped
    chives

2 teaspoons prepared
    mustard
½ teaspoon Worcestershire
    sauce
dash Tabasco
salt
buttered crumbs

Mix well all ingredients except buttered crumbs, and spread either in individual casseroles, on large scallop shells, or in a single shallow casserole. Top with thin layer of buttered crumbs and bake in hot oven, 400°, until well browned. Scallop shells will take about 10 minutes, individual casseroles about 15 minutes, and the single casserole about 20 minutes.   SERVES 3.

LOBSTER NEWBURG CANAPÉS

1 *cup LO lobster flaked*	1 *egg yolk lightly beaten*
2 *tablespoons butter*	2 *tablespoons sherry*
2 *tablespoons flour*	*rounds of bread toasted on*
¾ *cup top milk*	*one side*
salt and pepper	½ *cup grated American*
dash cayenne pepper	*cheese or 3 tablespoons*
¼ *teaspoon paprika*	*grated Parmesan cheese*

Served piping hot these are wonderful hors d'oeuvres. If you make the mixture with canned lobster, double the recipe and make a delicious luncheon dish, using half slices of bread with crusts removed.

Heat butter in skillet, blend in flour, cook for a moment, and stir in milk gradually, stirring constantly until thick and smooth. Season to taste with salt and pepper, cayenne pepper, and paprika. Stir a little of the hot sauce into the egg, and add egg mixture with lobster meat to sauce, stirring constantly until smooth and hot. Stir in sherry. Pile mixture on untoasted side of rounds of bread, arrange on baking sheet, top with cheese, and either bake 10–12 minutes in hot oven, 450°, or brown lightly under broiler until cheese is melted.

LOBSTER COCKTAIL

1 *cup LO lobster meat*
    diced
½ *cup heart of celery diced*
½ *cup crisp lettuce shredded*
3 *tablespoons mayonnaise*
1 *tablespoon chili sauce*
1 *teaspoon catsup*

1 *teaspoon Worcestershire*
    sauce
1 *small tomato peeled,*
    seeded, and chopped
    fine
½ *teaspoon chopped chives*
½ *teaspoon minced parsley*
    salt

Mix lobster, celery, and lettuce. Chill while you prepare
the dressing. Mix mayonnaise, chili sauce, catsup, Worcestershire sauce, tomato, chives, and parsley. Blend gently
with lobster mixture, add a little salt if needed, and serve
in crisp lettuce cups in sherbet glasses. Serves 4 as a first
course or 2 as a main course.

LOBSTER SALAD SANDWICHES

1 *cup LO lobster chopped*
1 *hard-cooked egg*
1 *small tomato peeled and*
    chopped

salt
2 *tablespoons mayonnaise*
buttered bread

Mix ingredients thoroughly, season to taste, and spread
rather generously on buttered white, whole wheat, or
pumpernickel bread. Top with second slices, press rather
firmly, trim crusts, and cut in halves, thirds, or quarters.
Makes enough to cover about 6 slices, depending on size.

Note: This mixture is also good as stuffing for small finger
rolls. Cut off top, scoop out most of soft center, and fill
with lobster mixture.

CHINESE FRIED LOBSTER

2 cups cooked lobster
    chopped fine
2 tablespoons cooking oil
¾ cup finely chopped onion
¼ cup minced celery
½ cup minced cucumber
¼ cup mushrooms minced

1 cup chicken broth or
    consommé
2 tablespoons butter or
    margarine
¼ cup sherry
salt and pepper
2 teaspoons flour
1 teaspoon soy sauce

Heat oil to sizzling and cook for 2 minutes the onion, celery, cucumber, and mushrooms, stirring constantly. Add chicken broth or consommé, reduce heat, cover, and simmer 3–4 minutes. While this is cooking heat half of the butter in another skillet and quickly but lightly sauté the lobster, just for 1 minute. Add sherry and simmer 2 minutes more. Combine the two mixtures and cook 3 minutes. Knead the remaining tablespoon of butter with the flour and stir into the mixture to thicken it. Season with salt and pepper to taste and soy sauce. A pleasant addition at this point, if on hand, is ½ cup cut-up bean sprouts. When piping hot serve with hot fluffy rice.   SERVES 4–5.

LOBSTER AU GRATIN

2 cups LO lobster meat cut
    up
½ cup sliced mushrooms
    sautéed
4 tablespoons butter
2 tablespoons flour
1½ cups light cream

½ teaspoon dry mustard
3 tablespoons grated Par-
    mesan cheese
salt
1 egg yolk lightly beaten
2 tablespoons sherry (opt.)

Make a cream sauce of 2 tablespoons of the butter, the flour, and the cream. Blend in mustard and 2 tablespoons cheese, simmer a moment, and season to taste. Mix a little of this sauce with the egg yolk, and stir quickly into the sauce. Add 1 tablespoon butter bit by bit. Combine with lobster meat and mushrooms. Add sherry. Pour into 5-cup casserole, sprinkle with remaining tablespoon of cheese, dot with remaining butter, and bake 15 minutes in 400° oven, or until well heated and brown on top.   SERVES 4.

LOBSTER-STUFFED EGGS—*Cold*

4 *hard-cooked eggs*	1 *teaspoon lemon juice*
½ *cup LO lobster meat*	*pinch of sweet basil or*
chopped fine	*chervil*
2 *tablespoons mayonnaise*	1½ *tablespoons soft butter*
½ *teaspoon salt*	

To hard-cook eggs cook about 12 minutes in water kept just under boiling. Turn them 2 or 3 times in the first 5 minutes to center the yolks. When done plunge at once into cold water to prevent the formation of a black line around the yolks.

Cut eggs in two lengthwise and carefully remove yolks to a bowl. Mix thoroughly with remaining ingredients, working to a soft smooth paste. Fill whites, extending filling to edges. Chill until firm. (The butter in the filling gives the chilled eggs a pleasantly firm texture.)

LOBSTER-STUFFED EGGS—*Hot*

Stuff the eggs exactly as in the preceding recipe, but omit butter. Arrange close together in shallow casserole or deep pie plate and cover with 1 cup cheese sauce, made with 2 tablespoons butter or margarine, 2 tablespoons flour, 1 cup milk, ½ cup grated cheese, and salt and pepper to taste. Sprinkle top with a little more grated cheese and bake 15–20 minutes at 375°, or until top is golden brown. SERVES 4.

LOBSTER TOAST

1 cup cooked lobster meat   1 tablespoon sherry
    diced small   ¼ cup blanched slivered
1 cup rich cream sauce   almonds
1 egg yolk lightly beaten   salt and pepper

Make the cream sauce with 2 tablespoons butter or margarine, 2 tablespoons flour, and 1 cup top milk or half milk,
half cream. Season to taste. Mix a little of the hot sauce
with the egg yolk and stir yolk quickly into sauce. Mix in
sherry, lobster, almonds, and a little salt and pepper if
needed. Serve on fresh buttered toast.   SERVES 3.

SHRIMP SPREAD

½ cup LO shrimp minced   pinch nutmeg
salt and pepper   2 teaspoons soft butter
dash of powdered mace

Leftover shrimp make a good spread, either for canapés to
serve with cocktails or for luncheon sandwiches.

Chop shrimp as fine as possible, and mash further with
wooden spoon. Mix well with remaining ingredients and
heat in saucepan until it begins to bubble, stirring constantly. Pack in small jars and chill. If you own an electric
blender, 30 seconds in that will produce a velvety smooth-
ness.

SHRIMP COCKTAIL

1 cup LO cooked and
    cleaned shrimp
½ cup mayonnaise
1 scant teaspoon prepared
    mustard
2 teaspoons minced
    gherkins

1 teaspoon chopped capers
1 teaspoon minced parsley
½ teaspoon chervil
½ teaspoon tarragon
anchovy paste size of a pea
salt and pepper

Mix well all ingredients except the shrimp, beating vigorously. Use salt and pepper with discretion—you may not need any at all. Mix dressing with shrimp, chill, and serve on bed of shredded lettuce in sherbet cups. Serves 4 as a first course or 2 as a main-course salad.

SHRIMP SANDWICHES

1 cup LO cooked shrimp
    minced
½ cup chopped cucumber
    drained
1 teaspoon chopped chives

1 tablespoon French
    dressing
1 tablespoon mayonnaise
salt
buttered bread

Blend ingredients well, season to taste, and spread quite generously on white, whole wheat, or pumpernickel bread. Add top slices, press together, and cut in halves, thirds, or quarters. Will spread about 6 slices.

Note: This mixture is also good used to stuff small finger rolls.

MARINATED SHRIMP

1 cup LO cooked and
   cleaned shrimp
¼ cup wine vinegar
¼ cup olive oil
½ medium garlic clove
   mashed

1 tablespoon chopped
   scallion (green onion)
½ teaspoon chili sauce
½ teaspoon prepared
   mustard
½ teaspoon salt

Blend ingredients well and toss shrimp in the mixture
enough to be sure that all are well coated. Let stand in
refrigerator several hours or overnight, stirring two or three
times. Serve on crisp lettuce leaves as a luncheon salad or
stuck on toothpicks as a cocktail accompaniment.

MOLD OF SHRIMP AND SALMON

1 cup LO salmon coarsely
   flaked
2 cups cooked shrimp
   chopped coarsely
1½ envelopes gelatin
1 cup dry white wine
2 cups hot consommé
1 scant tablespoon curry
   powder

salt and pepper
1 cup chopped celery
½ cup chopped canned
   pimiento
½ cup finely diced
   cucumber
1 large black truffle
   chopped (opt.)
1 cup heavy cream whipped

This is a delicious hot-weather dish, and with a little deco-
ration it becomes a fine party dish. If you have only salmon
or shrimp left over, open a tin of the other one to combine
with the other ingredients.

Make the gelatin part first. Soften gelatin in wine and
dissolve in hot consommé. Add curry powder mixed with a
few drops of water and salt and pepper to taste. Chill, and
also chill the mold you are going to use.

Mix salmon and shrimp lightly with celery, pimiento,
cucumber, and truffle if you use it. Let stand.

When gelatin mixture shows signs of thickening, pour some in the cold mold and roll mold to cover the surface completely. Put back in the refrigerator to set firmly and then add another layer of gelatin to the mold. Now add decorations if you want, pressing into the gelatin fancy shapes of green pepper, sliced hard-cooked egg, cucumber slices, bits of pimiento, sliced stuffed olives, or whatever strikes your fancy, dipping each piece into the slightly thickened gelatin before adding it to the mold. Chill.

Blend whipped cream with remaining gelatin, mix with salmon-shrimp mixture, fill mold, pressing down lightly but firmly, and chill until firm. Unmold on chilled platter and surround with crisp lettuce or watercress, quartered hard-cooked eggs, and black olives. Serve with a bowl of mayonnaise to which a little curry powder has been added.

SERVES 6–8.

SHRIMP-STUFFED TOMATOES

LO shrimp cut small   *capers*
French dressing   *small tomatoes*
mayonnaise

Plunge tomatoes into boiling water for a minute or two, slip off skins, scoop out insides, salt insides lightly, and turn upside down to drain. Add a few capers to the cut-up shrimp with the tomato pieces you have scooped out and chopped, mix with French dressing and mayonnaise blended half-and-half, and stuff tomatoes.

SCRAMBLED EGGS WITH SHRIMP

1 cup LO cooked shrimp
   broken in small pieces
6 eggs
3 tablespoons light cream
3 tablespoons butter or
   margarine

2 shallots minced (or 1
   teaspoon minced
   onion)
2 mushroom caps sliced
2 medium tomatoes peeled
   and chopped
salt and pepper

Beat eggs lightly with cream (just enough to blend smoothly) and let stand while preparing balance. Melt butter in skillet, add shallots and mushrooms, and simmer 4–5 minutes. Add tomato and shrimp and continue cooking until they are well heated through. Pour in eggs and stir gently until creamy. Season to taste and serve on fresh buttered toast.   SERVES 4–6.

VEGETABLES

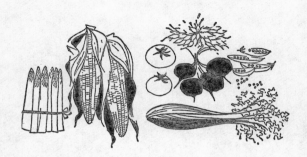

VEGETABLES

CREAMED ASPARAGUS AND EGGS

*LO cooked asparagus spears
    cut in 1-inch lengths
hard-cooked eggs sliced*

*cream sauce or cheese sauce
minced parsley*

Quantities here are very flexible, and will depend on how much asparagus you have left over. To about 1 cup of cut pieces use 2 or 3 hard-cooked eggs and 1½–2 cups of either rich cream sauce or cheese sauce. Make cream sauce with 3 tablespoons butter or margarine, 2 tablespoons flour, and 1½ cups whole milk. Season to taste. Add ½ cup grated cheese to this quantity if you want a cheese sauce. Heat asparagus and eggs in the sauce in a double boiler, stir in ½ teaspoon parsley, and serve over fresh buttered toast with a dash of paprika on top. This quantity will serve 4 quite generously.

STRING-BEAN SALAD

*LO cooked string beans
minced or grated onion
minced parsley*

*sweet basil or sweet
    marjoram
French dressing*

If you have only a few string beans left over, mix with a very little onion and parsley, basil, or marjoram. Blend with French dressing, chill for 15–30 minutes or longer, and add to a tossed green salad.

If you have a good quantity of string beans left over, proceed as above and serve on crisp lettuce leaves. If beans are whole cut in ¾-inch pieces or slit lengthwise (French them).

BAKED-BEAN SOUP

2 *cups LO baked beans*
1 *tablespoon bacon fat*
1 *medium onion sliced*
1 *small clove garlic minced*
1 *small green pepper*
   chopped
1 *cup chopped tomato*
   (fresh or canned)

2 *cups consommé*
1 *stalk celery cut up*
½ *teaspoon parsley chopped*
1 *small bay leaf*
salt and pepper
¼ *cup Madeira or sherry*

Melt bacon fat in small soup kettle and in it sauté onion, garlic, and green pepper until onion is yellow. Add tomato, consommé, beans, celery, parsley, and bay leaf. Bring to a boil, season to taste, lower heat, and simmer 30 minutes. Press through a sieve or put through a food mill. Reheat, add Madeira or sherry, and serve with a thin slice of lemon dusted with paprika and finely minced parsley in each plate. Serves 4–6, depending upon whether served in cups or plates.

HOT BAKED-BEAN SANDWICHES

1 *cup LO baked beans*
   mashed
1 *teaspoon minced onion*
¼ *teaspoon prepared*
   mustard

2 *tablespoons mayonnaise*
salt
softened butter
bread

Anyone who likes baked beans will find these sandwiches a treat to look forward to when home-baked beans are left over. With a green salad they make a fine lunch.

To the mashed beans add onion, mustard, mayonnaise, and salt if needed. Spread slice of bread very generously with this mixture, cover with top slice, press together firmly, and spread both top and bottom of sandwich evenly but thinly with softened butter. Heat heavy skillet (preferably cast iron) to sizzling, lay in sandwiches, lower heat, and brown slowly on both sides. Serve at once while they are piping hot. This quantity of beans will make about 4 good-sized sandwiches.

BEET SALAD

LO *cooked beets*   *fresh dill if available*
thin slices of white onions *salt and pepper*
chervil   *French dressing*

In France the only vegetable one commonly finds added to a tossed green salad is julienne strips of cooked beets. If you have enough cooked beets on hand to make a salad, however, blend *sliced* beets with about half the same quantity of onion slices, a good pinch of chervil and fresh dill, salt and pepper to taste, and enough "herby" French dressing to moisten well. Chill and serve on crisp lettuce leaves.

BEET AND CELERY SALAD

LO *cooked beets cut in* *double the amount of water-*
 julienne strips   *cress leaves (stems re-*
equal amount of celery cut *moved)*
 in same-size strips *French dressing*

This is a simple and good salad. Have ingredients well chilled before mixing and toss with just enough French dressing to coat pieces.

CHIFFONADE SALAD

½ cup chopped LO beets
½ cup romaine torn in
    pieces, ribs removed
½ cup crisp lettuce torn in
    strips
½ cup chicory torn in pieces
½ cup julienne strips of
    celery

1 small tomato peeled and
    cut in thin wedges
2 hard-cooked eggs
    chopped
½ cup watercress, stems
    removed
French dressing

This delicious salad is a standard luncheon dish with many
fine restaurants, and is a fine solution to the problem of
leftover beets.

Mix all ingredients lightly in a large bowl and toss with
just enough French dressing to be sure that all pieces are
coated. If you have dressing left in the bottom of the bowl
this is a sure sign you have used too much dressing.

SERVES 6–8.

CABBAGE AU GRATIN

2 cups LO boiled cabbage
    chopped
1 cup medium cream sauce
½ cup plus 1 tablespoon
    grated cheese

1 tablespoon rum (opt.)
2 tablespoons buttered
    crumbs

This recipe rings such a pleasant change on plain boiled
cabbage that it justifies cooking much more cabbage than
your family will eat, to give you the "makings" of this
casserole.

Make the cream sauce with 2 tablespoons butter or margarine, 2 tablespoons flour, 1 cup of milk, and salt and
pepper to taste. Mix cabbage (well drained), cream sauce,
the ½ cup of cheese, and the rum. Put in a casserole, and
top with crumbs mixed with the tablespoon of cheese. Bake

in moderate oven, 350°, about 15 minutes, or until well browned. SERVES 5–6.

CARROT RING

2 cups LO carrots mashed
    or riced
2 tablespoons butter or
    margarine melted

salt and pepper
2 teaspoons minced onion
4 eggs well beaten
1 cup milk

Mix ingredients well and turn into well-greased ring mold. Set in pan of hot water and bake in moderate oven, 350°, about 40 minutes, or until top is firm to the touch. Let stand 2–3 minutes before unmolding. Loosen edges and unmold on heated platter. Fill center with buttered green peas or Frenched string beans. Or use center for creamed salmon or tuna. SERVES 6–8.

CAULIFLOWER SOUFFLÉ

1–2 cups LO cauliflower
    flowerets
2 medium tomatoes skinned
    and sliced
3 tablespoons flour
3 tablespoons butter or
    margarine

2 cups milk
1 cup grated sharp cheese
salt and pepper
dash of cayenne pepper
3 eggs separated
2 tablespoons buttered
    bread crumbs

Break up the cauliflower into quite small pieces. In a well-greased 6-cup casserole or soufflé dish arrange alternate layers of cauliflower pieces and tomato slices. Make a cream sauce of the flour, butter, and milk. When it is thick and smooth add cheese and stir constantly until melted. Remove from heat, season to taste, and add well-beaten egg yolks. Cool to lukewarm and fold in egg whites beaten until stiff but not dry. Pour gently over cauliflower and tomato in casserole, top with buttered crumbs, and bake in moderate oven, 375°, 30–35 minutes, or until knife inserted in center comes out clean. SERVES 4–5.

CORN PANCAKES

1 *cup LO boiled corn cut*
   from cob
1 *cup sifted all-purpose*
   flour
1½ *teaspoons baking powder*
½ *teaspoon salt*

¼ *teaspoon paprika*
1 *egg well beaten*
½ *cup milk*
2 *tablespoons melted butter*
   or margarine

Leftover green corn makes wonderful pancakes for a luncheon dish. Or make large pancakes, butter generously, pile on top of each other, keeping warm, and cut in pie-shaped wedges to serve instead of potato with fried chicken. This recipe makes tender pancakes, but you can use a prepared pancake flour if you prefer, *adding to it both the egg and the melted shortening.*

Mix and sift dry ingredients. Combine egg, milk, and butter, and stir in. (If mixture is rather stiff add enough more milk to make it thin enough so that you can pour it from a pitcher.) Stir in corn and bake on hot greased griddle. Makes about a dozen medium pancakes.

BROILED CORN

2 *cups corn cut off the cobs*
   of LO boiled ears
1 *tablespoon minced onion*
salt and pepper

1 *tablespoon butter*
1½ *tablespoons grated*
   cheese

Cut kernels off the ears with a sharp knife, and run the back of the knife down the cobs to get all the milky part. If corn seems quite dry add a tablespoon or so of cream. Mix with onion and salt and pepper to taste. Spread in greased shallow casserole or Pyrex pie plate, top with dabs of butter and cheese, and brown lightly under broiler flame, keeping casserole two inches from flame.   SERVES 4–5.

CORN FRITTERS

1 *cup corn cut from LO*
   corn-on-the-cob
2 *eggs well beaten*
½ *teaspoon salt*

1 *teaspoon double-action*
   baking powder
1 *cup flour*
fat for frying

Cut corn from cobs with a sharp knife, and scrape cob to get all the milk. Stir in eggs. Mix baking powder with flour and salt and stir into corn mixture. Drop by tablespoonfuls into either deep fat heated to 375° or an inch of fat heated in a heavy skillet. Fry to golden brown on both sides and drain on brown paper or paper towels. Makes 10–12 fritters, depending on size.

CORN PIE

2 *cups corn cut from LO*
   boiled ears
½ *pound bacon*
¼ *cup chopped green*
   pepper
¼ *cup chopped onion*

3 *hard-cooked eggs*
   chopped
1 *can condensed cream of*
   mushroom soup
½ *teaspoon salt*
pastry

Roll out pastry for two-crust pie and line shallow casserole or Pyrex pie plate. Cook bacon until crisp. Drain, crumble, and mix with remaining ingredients. Pour corn mixture into crust, top with top crust, well slashed to permit steam to escape, and bake 45–50 minutes in hot oven, 400°.

SERVES 6.

GREEN CORN SOUFFLÉ

1 *cup LO corn cut from the*   *dash paprika*
  cobs   2 *tablespoons butter or*
3 *eggs separated*   *margarine*
½ *teaspoon salt*

Beat egg yolks until thick and add corn, salt, and paprika.
Heat shallow casserole in oven with butter in it. While it
is heating fold stiffly beaten egg whites into the corn mixture. Pour gently into hot casserole and bake 25 minutes
in moderate oven, 350°, or until knife thrust into the center
comes out clean. Serve with cheese sauce.   SERVES 4.

CORN-STUFFED GREEN PEPPERS

2 *cups corn cut off the cobs*   2 *tablespoons sugar*
  of LO boiled ears   2 *teaspoons onion salt*
6 *medium green peppers*   2 *tablespoons bread crumbs*
½ *cup thin cream sauce*   2 *tablespoons grated cheese*
¼ *cup tomato catsup*   2 *tablespoons butter*

Cut kernels off ears of corn with a sharp knife, and run
the back of the knife down the cobs to get all the milky
part. Cut tops off peppers, remove seeds and membranes
carefully, and parboil both peppers and tops in salted boiling water 2–3 minutes, or until somewhat tender but not
soft. Cut tops in small pieces and mix with corn, cream
sauce (made with 2 teaspoons butter or margarine, 2 teaspoons flour, ½ cup milk, and seasoning to taste), catsup,
sugar, and onion salt. Stand the pepper cases in a greased
shallow casserole and fill them with the corn mixture. Top
with bread crumbs, then cheese, and then dabs of butter.
Add about 2 tablespoons of water in the bottom of the casserole and bake in a hot oven, 400°, 12–15 minutes, or
until tops are well browned.   SERVES 6.

PEAS WITH BRAISED CELERY

1 *cup LO cooked peas*
   (or more)
3 *cups celery cut in ⅛-inch*
   pieces
2 *tablespoons butter or*
   margarine

2 *tablespoons minced onion*
½ *cup consommé or chicken*
   broth
3 *tablespoons heavy cream*
salt to taste

This combination of flavors is such a "natural" that it even warrants having peas cooked especially for it!

Melt fat in heavy skillet, cook onions a moment or two, and turn in celery. Cook until celery shows touch of color, then add consommé, cover skillet, and simmer over lowest possible heat 20–25 minutes, stirring once or twice. Add a bit more consommé if dry. Stir in peas and cream, salt to taste, and just heat through. Serve at once. SERVES 5–6.

POTATO SOUP

2 *cups LO boiled potatoes*
   diced, or mashed
   potatoes
1 *medium onion coarsely*
   chopped

3 *cups milk*
1 *tablespoon butter or*
   margarine
salt and pepper
chopped parsley

Potato soup is of course better if made with raw potatoes, but leftover potatoes can be utilized to make a very good soup.

Cover onion with water and cook gently, covered, until soft, and water is almost gone. Just before it is done stir in the potato dice or mashed potato, and continue cooking until they are well heated. Heat milk with butter, and when it is hot but not scalded put onion and potato through a sieve or food mill and stir in. Add salt and pepper to taste and simmer over very low heat, not allowing it to boil, about 5 minutes. Sprinkle each plate with parsley before serving. If you have a leftover frankfurter or a couple of Vienna sausages on hand, cut them into rather thin circles and add just before soup is ready to serve. Serves 4–6, depending upon whether served in plates or cups.

AU GRATIN POTATOES

3 *cups LO baked or boiled potatoes cut in small dice*
2 *cups cream sauce*

1–1½ *cups grated cheese*
1 *tablespoon butter*
dash of paprika

Au gratin potatoes seem to have much more flavor if the potatoes are cut in very small cubes, even as small as ¼ inch. Make the cream sauce rather thin—2 tablespoons butter or margarine, 2 tablespoons flour, and 2 cups milk. Cook until smooth and thickened, season to taste (more if potatoes are not well seasoned), and melt all but about 2 tablespoons of the cheese in it. Taste critically, and add more cheese if necessary, as it will be if the cheese is rather bland. Stir in potatoes well, turn into 4-cup casserole, sprinkle top with reserved cheese, dot with butter, and sprinkle with a little paprika. Bake in 400° oven 15–20 minutes, or until top is golden brown.   SERVES 6.

BAKED POTATO OMELET

5 *medium LO boiled potatoes cut in ½-inch dice*
5 *eggs well beaten*
3 *strips bacon cut in 1-inch pieces*

1 *tablespoon bacon fat*
1 *medium onion sliced*
½ *teaspoon caraway seed (opt.)*
salt and pepper

This is a hearty and flavorful dish for lunch or Sunday-night supper. The caraway seed adds a distinctive flavor, but you can do without it.

Put the bacon pieces, bacon fat, and onion in a large

heavy skillet, preferably cast iron, and cook until onion begins to color. Add potatoes and caraway seed, stir well to coat, and sauté until golden brown, stirring frequently. Add salt and pepper to taste to the eggs and pour gently over the potatoes. Do not stir, but cook 2–3 minutes until eggs are set on the bottom. Then set skillet in a medium oven, 375°, and bake until eggs are set on the top. Cut in pie-shaped pieces and remove to heated platter. Or cook the whole thing in a shallow casserole that has been heat-proofed and serve at the table. SERVES 6.

CHEESE-CREAMED POTATOES

3 cups LO boiled or baked   2 cups cream sauce
   potatoes cut in ½-inch   ¾ cup grated cheese,
   dice   American or Cheddar

Leftover baked potatoes are better for creaming than boiled. Either is improved when the sauce is cheese sauce.

Make the cream sauce rather thin—2 tablespoons butter or margarine, 2 scant tablespoons flour, and 2 cups of milk. Cook until smooth and thickened, season to taste, and stir in cheese. When cheese is melted add potatoes and heat well, but not to boiling. SERVES 6.

CREAMED POTATOES

6 medium LO boiled   1 cup thin cream or top
   potatoes cut in ½-inch   milk
   dice   salt and pepper
2 tablespoons butter or   1 tablespoon chopped
   margarine   parsley

This is certainly the simplest of all ways to utilize leftover boiled potatoes, but don't try to make it with plain milk, because it won't thicken.

Melt butter in skillet, stir in potatoes until they are well coated, cover with cream or top milk, season to taste, cover,

and simmer over very low heat until sauce is partly absorbed and somewhat thickened. Turn into hot serving dish
and sprinkle with parsley.   SERVES 5.

CREAMED POTATOES AND PEAS

6 *medium LO boiled po-*   salt
   tatoes cut in ½-inch   1 *cup LO cooked green*
   dice   *peas*
2 *cups cream sauce*

Make cream sauce with 3 tablespoons butter or margarine,
3 tablespoons flour, and 2 cups milk. Season to taste, combine with potatoes and peas, turn into double boiler, and
heat over boiling water until well heated, stirring occasionally.   SERVES 5–6.

LYONNAISE POTATOES

6 *medium LO boiled*   3 *tablespoons bacon fat*
   potatoes cut in ½-inch   *salt and pepper*
   dice or smaller   1 *cup chopped onion*

Heat fat to sizzling in heavy skillet and turn in potatoes.
Sprinkle with salt and pepper if potatoes are not well seasoned. As they start to cook stir in onion. Cover, reduce
heat to very low, and cook 15–20 minutes, stirring occasionally. Uncover the last 5 minutes.   SERVES 6.
   Some people sprinkle 2 or more tablespoons of tarragon
or wine vinegar over the top of this quantity of potatoes
just before serving.

Note: If you add 2–3 tablespoons of chopped pimiento toward the end of the cooking time Lyonnaise potatoes become O'Brien potatoes.

GEORGIA BAKED SWEET POTATOES

2 cups LO sweet potatoes
    mashed
salt
dash of nutmeg

¼ cup corn syrup and
    molasses mixed
2 tablespoons butter

Spread potatoes in small greased casserole, sprinkle with salt and nutmeg, pour syrup over, dot with butter, and bake in 350° oven until brown, about 30 minutes.   SERVES 4.

HAWAIIAN SWEET POTATOES

LO sweet potatoes, baked,
    boiled, mashed, or
    candied
salt and pepper

butter or margarine
canned crushed pineapple,
    well drained
pecan halves

Mash well and season to taste any quantity of cooked sweet potatoes you have left over. Add butter and pineapple in the proportions of 1 tablespoon butter and ¼ cup pineapple to every cup of mashed potato. Spread in shallow greased casserole, arrange pecan halves on top, and bake 10–15 minutes in moderate oven, 350°. Slide under broiler a moment to brown top.

GERMAN POTATO SALAD

2 cups LO boiled potatoes
    sliced
1 teaspoon sugar
½ teaspoon salt
¼ teaspoon dry mustard

2 tablespoons mild vinegar
1 cup sour cream
½ cup thinly sliced
    cucumber
paprika

This salad is particularly good when made with tiny new

potatoes which have been boiled in their jackets. If you have these on hand do not peel them.

Mix sugar, salt, mustard, and vinegar and stir into sour cream. Add cucumber to potatoes and gently stir in the dressing until potatoes are well coated. Sprinkle with paprika and serve at room temperature.   SERVES 4–5.

POTATO CAKES

1½ cups LO mashed
    potatoes
1 teaspoon minced parsley,
    chives, or tops of green
    onions (scallions)
    chopped (opt.)

1 egg well beaten
2 tablespoons melted butter
    or margarine
2 tablespoons bacon fat

The addition of finely chopped greens to mashed potatoes is a nice touch.

Mix well cold potatoes, greens, egg, and melted butter. If potatoes are not well seasoned add a little salt and pepper. Mold with the hands into flat cakes ½–¾ inches thick (flour your hands if the potatoes stick), and sauté to a golden brown on both sides in sizzling bacon fat or butter.
                                                    SERVES 4.

POTATO SOUFFLÉ

2 cups LO mashed potatoes
½ cup light cream
salt
pinch nutmeg

2 tablespoons grated Par-
    mesan or Swiss cheese
3 egg yolks
4 egg whites beaten stiff

Mix potatoes thoroughly with cream, season to taste, and add nutmeg. Cook over very low heat until hot, or heat in double boiler. Remove from heat, stir in cheese, and beat in egg yolks, one at a time, beating hard after each addition. Cool to lukewarm and fold in egg whites. Fill a deep well-greased casserole ¾ full and bake in moderate oven,

375°, 30–35 minutes, or until soufflé is well puffed and delicately brown. Serve at once.   SERVES 6.

POTATO-TUNA SALAD

3–4 *small LO boiled po-*
   tatoes sliced rather thin
1 *large can tuna broken in*
   coarse chunks
heart leaves of 2 heads of
   romaine torn in pieces,
   ribs removed
1 *head curly endive torn in*
   pieces

1 *large bunch watercress*
   with stems removed
1 *small green pepper cut in*
   julienne strips
3 *small tomatoes peeled and*
   cut in thin wedges
French dressing

Mix all ingredients and toss lightly with just enough French dressing to coat the pieces. This salad is improved if all ingredients are well chilled when you start to mix it.

SERVES 5–6.

QUICK SCALLOPED POTATOES

4 *cups LO boiled potatoes*
   sliced

2 *cups cream sauce*
1 *tablespoon butter*

Make a rather thin cream sauce, with 2 tablespoons butter or margarine, 2 tablespoons flour, and 2 cups milk. Cook until smooth and rather thick, season to taste, and stir in potatoes. Continue to cook until well heated. Turn into greased casserole, top with dabs of butter, and bake about 15–20 minutes in a hot oven, 400°, until golden brown on top.   SERVES 6–8.

SWEET POTATO CROQUETTES

2 cups riced LO cooked
    sweet potatoes
¼ cup melted butter
2 teaspoons salt
¼ cup brown sugar
¼ teaspoon black pepper

½ cup chopped nuts,
    preferably almonds
    blanched and toasted
fine bread crumbs
1 egg
1 tablespoon water
fat for deep frying

Any kind of cooked sweet potatoes can be used here—
mashed, boiled, glazed, or candied. If you use glazed or
candied potatoes use only half as much brown sugar as
called for. Mix vigorously with butter, salt, sugar, pepper,
and nuts. Shape into croquettes the size and shape of fat
sausages. Beat egg lightly with water. Put crumbs in one
soup plate and egg in another. Roll croquettes carefully,
first in crumbs, then in egg, and then in crumbs again.
Chill. Fry in deep fat heated to 385° until golden brown
and drain on brown paper or paper towels. Makes about
10 small croquettes, serving 5.

Note: If potato mixture is too soft to handle easily, chill
before shaping into croquettes and again after coating
them.

SWEET POTATO SOUFFLÉ I

2 cups LO sweet potatoes
½ cup hot milk
¼ cup brandy (scant)
4 tablespoons melted butter
    or margarine
dash cayenne pepper

pinch nutmeg
½ teaspoon salt
1 teaspoon grated lemon
    rind
4 eggs separated

Leftover mashed yams or sweet potatoes are best for this
dish, but candied yams or sweet potatoes that have been

fixed with crushed pineapple will also work well. In the last
two cases omit butter from this recipe.

Beat potatoes vigorously, stirring in milk, brandy, and
melted butter. When mixture is smooth add remaining seasonings and well-beaten egg yolks. Fold in stiffly beaten
whites, turn into well-greased casserole, and bake in hot
oven, 400°, 25–30 minutes, or until well puffed and lightly
browned.   SERVES 5–6.

SWEET POTATO SOUFFLÉ II

2 *cups LO sweet potatoes*
  mashed
¾ *teaspoon salt*
2 *cups rich milk or thin*
  cream
2 *tablespoons cornstarch*

½ *cup honey or ¼ cup brown*
  sugar
3 *eggs well beaten*
1 *cup pecans coarsely*
  chopped

Whip potatoes hard, in electric mixer if possible. Add salt,
milk or cream, cornstarch dissolved in a little of the milk,
honey or brown sugar, eggs, and pecans. Or save out 2
tablespoons of the pecans to spread on the top. Beat well
again, pour in greased 6-cup casserole and bake in 325°
oven about 40 minutes, or until firm. If you want to make
this still richer, add a topping of marshmallows the last 10
minutes and put all the nuts into the potatoes. Be warned,
however, that this makes a pretty deadly dish! SERVES 8.

TOLL HOUSE HOT POTATO SALAD

3 *cups LO boiled potatoes*
  cut in small dice
French dressing

½ *cup cream sauce*
½ *cup mayonnaise*
1 *medium onion chopped*
  fine

The addition of mayonnaise to the cream sauce makes a
wonderful hot potato salad, and one very simple to make.
Stir enough French dressing into the potatoes just to

moisten them, and let stand, from half an hour to all day.
Make cream sauce with 1 tablespoon butter or margarine,
1 tablespoon flour, and ½ cup milk. Season to taste, stir in
mayonnaise and onion, blend with potatoes, and spread in
shallow casserole. Bake in hot oven, 400°, 15–20 minutes,
long enough to brown slightly.   SERVES 6.

SPINACH TIMBALES

1 *cup LO spinach*
1 *teaspoon onion juice or
   grated onion*
3 *eggs well beaten*

2 *tablespoons melted butter
   or margarine*
1 *cup milk*
salt and pepper

Spinach for timbales must be very dry to start with. Chop
as fine as possible or force through a fine sieve or food mill
and drain again through fine sieve. Mix with remaining ingredients and turn into well-greased custard cups. Set in
pan of hot water and bake in moderate oven, 350°, about
30 minutes, or until firm to the touch. Let stand about 2
minutes after removing from oven and unmold. Serve with
tomato or cheese sauce.   SERVES 6.

MIXED LEFTOVER VEGETABLES

The combination of corn and lima beans known as succo-
tash is well known to Americans, but many other combinations are equally good. Reheat in a double boiler with a
little butter or margarine, a little cream, or enough sour
cream to moisten well. Among the better mixtures are the
following:

creamed carrots and braised celery
creamed carrots and chopped spinach
creamed celery and green peas
string beans and mushrooms
string beans and creamed white onions
green lima beans and peas

whole-kernel corn (or corn cut from cob) and peas
cauliflower flowerets and green peas
breaded sautéed eggplant and stewed tomatoes
a few thinly sliced or shredded mushrooms with almost
   any of these combinations
carrots, cut string beans, green peas, lima beans, whole-
   kernel corn, braised celery, or any combination of these
   heated together

VEGETABLE FONDUE

2 cups LO cooked vegeta-
   bles: peas, cut green
   beans, lima beans,
   diced or sliced carrots,
   whole-kernel corn, or
   any mixture of them
2 cups whole milk

2 eggs well beaten
1–2 tablespoons minced
   onion
1 cup grated cheese
2 cups soft bread crumbs
salt
paprika

If you have only 1 cup of leftover odds and ends of vegetables, open a small can of whole-kernel corn to piece out.
Or slice and sauté lightly a large onion. Or add sliced leftover or fresh-boiled potatoes.

In top part of double boiler mix milk, eggs, onion, cheese,
and bread crumbs. Cook over boiling water until cheese is
melted. Season to taste, stir in vegetables, and pour in shallow greased casserole. Dust top with paprika and bake in
moderate oven, 325°, about 30 minutes, or until firm.

SERVES 4–5.

VEGETABLE SOUFFLÉ RING

3 cups LO mixed vegetables
1 cup stock (meat, fish, poultry, or vegetable, depending on filling) or milk
3 eggs separated
½ cup milk
½ cup fine bread crumbs

2 teaspoons lemon juice
2 teaspoons onion juice or grated onion
pinch nutmeg
salt and pepper
creamed meat, fish, chicken, or mushrooms for center of ring

Cook vegetables in stock or milk for about 15 minutes, or until liquid is almost evaporated. Rub the whole thing through a fine sieve or food mill. Into the pulp stir well-beaten egg yolks, milk, bread crumbs, lemon juice, onion juice, nutmeg, and salt and pepper to taste. Blend well, cool to lukewarm, and fold in egg whites beaten until stiff with a few grains of salt. Pour gently into well-greased ring mold and bake in a hot oven, 400°, 30–35 minutes, or until top is firm to the touch. Let stand a moment before unmolding on a heated platter. Fill center with creamed meat, fish, chicken, or mushrooms.   SERVES 6–8.

MISCELLANEOUS

MISCELLANEOUS

MACARONI SALAD

2 cups cold cooked
   macaroni
2 tablespoons minced
   parsley
2 tablespoons minced
   green pepper
½ cup thinly sliced celery

¾ cup chopped LO cooked
   meat or 2 hard-cooked
   eggs sliced (opt.)
French dressing
2 tablespoons mayonnaise
2 tablespoons sour cream
1 teaspoon catsup

When you make macaroni and cheese, cook some extra macaroni for this delicious luncheon or supper dish. Or if you have baked macaroni and cheese left over, put it in a colander or coarse sieve and wash it thoroughly to remove sauce in which it was baked.

If pieces are rather long, chop macaroni lightly. Mix with parsley, green pepper, celery, and meat or eggs. Blend with enough French dressing just to coat the macaroni well and let stand an hour or so. At serving time blend mayonnaise, sour cream, and catsup and mix well with salad. SERVES 4.

RICE CAKES

2 cups cooked rice
1 egg well beaten
3–4 tablespoons dry sherry

salt and pepper to taste
dash of nutmeg
3 tablespoons butter

Mix rice with egg, sherry, salt and pepper, and nutmeg. Shape into flat cakes, chill briefly, and sauté to golden brown on both sides in sizzling butter. Don't skimp on the butter or rice will stick to pan. SERVES 4–6.

CHINESE FRIED RICE

2 cups cold LO boiled rice 2 tablespoons soy sauce
2 slices bacon diced small   salt and pepper
3 eggs well beaten

This is a versatile dish. Instead of bacon you can use 1–2
tablespoons bacon fat and ½–¾ cup of chopped leftover
chicken, beef, pork, ham, lobster, or crab. Or you can use
cooking oil instead of bacon fat. Any combination produces
a flavorsome dish.

Cook bacon in a skillet until crisp. Skim out the pieces
and reserve. Add rice to skillet and sauté over medium heat
about 5 minutes, stirring constantly. Add bacon bits and
eggs and continue to cook, stirring constantly, until eggs
are set. Season with soy sauce, a little pepper, and salt if
needed. Serve at once.   SERVES 4–5.

SPANISH RICE

3 cups LO boiled rice   ¼ cup green pepper
3 tablespoons butter or   chopped
    margarine   1¼ cups canned tomatoes
1 small onion chopped   salt and pepper

Melt butter in skillet and sauté onion and green pepper until onion begins to show color. Add tomatoes and rice, season to taste, heat to boiling, reduce heat, and simmer 5
minutes. Or turn into a casserole, cover with a fairly thick
layer of buttered bread crumbs, and bake 15 minutes in a
hot oven, 400°.   SERVES 5–6.

BAKED MILK TOAST

slices of stale white bread   hot milk (not scalded)
    about ½ inch thick   salt
butter

Stale bread here makes a delicious soufflé-like luncheon
dish with a minimum of work. Trim crusts from bread, toast
to a golden brown, and butter generously. Lay in well-
buttered shallow casserole or pie plate, cutting the pieces to
fit snugly. Salt the milk lightly and pour over toast slowly,
enough to just reach top surface. Cover and bake about
20 minutes in hot oven, 400°. Uncover the last 5 minutes
to let the top crisp.

CHEESE FRENCH TOAST

8 slices stale bread   2 eggs slightly beaten
slices of sharp Cheddar   ¼ cup milk
    cheese enough to cover   ½ teaspoon salt
    4 slices of bread   2 tablespoons butter, mar-
softened butter   garine, or cooking oil
salt

Stale bread is here turned into a delicious luncheon dish.
    Spread bread fairly generously with softened butter.
Cover 4 slices with cheese, top with remaining slices, and
press firmly together. Mix eggs, milk, and salt and pour in
flat soup plate. Dip sandwiches in, moistening both sides
well. Heat fat in heavy skillet and brown sandwiches slowly
to golden brown on each side. (They will be easier to handle if you cut each one in two before dipping.) Serve at
once.   SERVES 4.

DESSERTS

DESSERTS

BLUEBERRY BETTY

4 cups blueberries
2 cups stale bread cut in
   very small cubes
⅓ cup melted butter or
   margarine

½ cup brown sugar
2 tablespoons lemon juice
⅛ teaspoon salt
¼ cup bread crumbs

This is a pleasant variation on the familiar Brown Betty.
Dribble the melted butter over the bread cubes and stir
well to distribute the butter. Arrange half in a greased casserole and cover with half of the berries, half of the brown
sugar, half of the lemon juice, and a dash of salt. Repeat
the layers and top with bread crumbs. Cover and bake in a
moderate oven (350°) about 40 minutes. Uncover the last
15 minutes to brown the top. Serve warm but not hot with
either whipped cream or hard sauce. Or serve it "à la
mode," with a scoop of ice cream on top.   SERVES 6.

CHOCOLATE BREAD PUDDING

2 cups bread crumbs made
   from stale but not dry
   bread
2 squares bitter chocolate
   (2 ounces)
1 quart milk

2 tablespoons butter
2 eggs well beaten
⅓ cup sugar
¼ teaspoon salt
1 teaspoon vanilla

Melt chocolate and butter in top of double boiler over boiling water and stir in milk. Cook until milk is hot, then pour
over bread crumbs and let stand about 10 minutes. Mix
eggs, sugar, salt, and vanilla. When sugar is dissolved stir

into chocolate mixture. Pour into greased casserole, set in
pan of hot water, and bake in moderate oven, 350°, 50–60
minutes, or until a knife inserted in center comes out clean.
Serve hot with cream or ice cream, or chill and serve cold.

SERVES 8.

CARAMEL BREAD PUDDING

4 *slices stale bread, crusts removed, spread on both sides with softened butter or margarine, and cut in small cubes*
1 *quart milk*

¾ *cup brown sugar*
¼ *teaspoon salt*
2 *tablespoons butter or margarine*
3 *eggs well beaten*
1 *teaspoon vanilla*

Scald milk in top of double boiler, over boiling water, with
brown sugar, salt, and butter. Gradually pour a little of this
hot mixture over the eggs and stir rapidly. Add to milk in
double boiler and cook until somewhat thickened, stirring
constantly. Remove from stove and stir in vanilla. Put buttered bread cubes in 6-cup greased casserole and pour custard over. Set in pan of hot water and bake 50–60 minutes
in moderate oven, 350°, until firm in the center, or until a
knife inserted in center will come out clean. Serve warm or
cold, either plain or with cream or ice cream. SERVES 8.

APPLE BREAD PUDDING

8 *slices stale white bread,*
   crusts removed
3 *medium green apples*
   peeled and sliced
4 *eggs*
1 *cup sugar*
½ *cup melted butter or*
   margarine

½ *teaspoon grated nutmeg*
1 *teaspoon vanilla*
1 *quart milk*
1 *cup seedless raisins*
¼ *teaspoon cream of tartar*
6 *tablespoons confectioners'*
   sugar

Grease a large casserole generously and line it with half of
the bread slices, cutting and trimming them to fit. Separate
3 of the eggs. Beat the yolks with the whole egg until light
and then beat in the sugar. Add melted fat, nutmeg, vanilla,
and milk. Build up the casserole with a layer of half the
apples, half the raisins, and 2 slices of bread cut in pieces
to fit. Repeat the layers and pour over all of the egg mixture. Set in a pan of hot water and bake about 30 minutes
in a moderate oven, 350°. Remove from oven and cover
with a meringue made from the 3 egg whites beaten until
stiff but not dry with cream of tartar and confectioners'
sugar. Lower heat to 300° and return pudding to oven for
about 20 minutes, or until meringue is a delicate brown.
Serve either warm or cold.   SERVES 8.

SWEDISH APPLE BREAD PUDDING

4 *cups bread crumbs made*
from stale but not dry
bread (about ½ loaf)
8 *tart apples peeled, cored,*
and quartered
juice and grated rind of 1
lemon
rind of 1 orange grated
sugar
¼ *pound butter or*
margarine

½ *cup crumbs of hard*
crackers
Sauce for Pudding
4 *egg yolks*
sugar
2 *cups whipping*
cream
¼ *cup brandy*
1 *teaspoon vanilla*

The sauce for this pudding should be made the day before
and served very cold over the hot pudding. To make it,
beat the egg yolks hard and then beat in as much sugar
as they will take. Let cream come to quick boil and pour
gradually over egg mixture, stirring constantly. Let sauce
barely come to a boil, lift off and shake gently, and repeat
two or three times. Remove from stove, stir in vanilla and
brandy, and chill for a full day.

To make the pudding cook the apples with lemon juice,
lemon rind, orange rind, and a little sugar. Cook until apples are soft and add more sugar to taste, but it should
not be very sweet. Beat apples until you have a smooth
apple sauce. Melt butter in large skillet and lightly sauté
the bread crumbs. Butter a casserole well. Cover bottom
with half of the cracker crumbs. Add about ¾ inch of buttered bread crumbs, 1 inch of apple sauce, another layer
of crumbs, and the balance of the apple sauce. Top with
remaining cracker crumbs. Bake 1 hour in slow oven, 300°,
or until firm to the touch. Serve hot with cold sauce.

SERVES 6.

COCONUT BREAD PUDDING

1½ *cups stale bread cut in*   ½ *teaspoon almond extract*
    ½-*inch cubes*   2 *eggs slightly beaten*
3 *cups milk scalded*   1¼ *cups dry coconut lightly*
2 *tablespoons melted butter*   *toasted in* 350° *oven*
    or margarine   *jam or jelly*
½ *cup sugar*   2 *egg whites beaten stiff*
¼ *teaspoon salt*   4 *tablespoons confectioners'*
½ *teaspoon vanilla*   *sugar*

Combine bread cubes, milk, and butter and pour in greased casserole. Combine in a bowl the sugar, salt, vanilla, almond extract, and eggs. Stir into bread and milk mixture until well blended. Lightly stir in 1 cup of the coconut. Let casserole stand 5–10 minutes and then set in pan of hot water and bake in 350° oven 30–35 minutes, or until firm. Remove from oven, spread with ¼-inch layer of any jam or jelly, but preferably red, and top with meringue made of egg whites beaten with confectioners' sugar. Sprinkle with remaining coconut and return to oven for an additional 15 minutes, or until delicately browned. Serve warm or cold.

CRANBERRY CRISP

3 *cups bread crumbs made*   ½ *cup melted butter or*
    from stale but not dry   *margarine*
    bread   1 *egg yolk*
2 *cups cranberries*   2 *tablespoons sugar*
1 *cup sugar*   1 *cup cream whipped*
½ *cup orange juice*   1 *teaspoon vanilla*
½ *teaspoon cinnamon*

Put sugar, orange juice, and cinnamon in a saucepan and bring to a boil. Add cranberries and cook over medium heat about 2 minutes, or until berries begin to soften. Mix melted butter and bread crumbs thoroughly. In a greased casserole arrange alternate layers of crumbs and berries, ending with layer of crumbs. Cover and bake in moderate oven, 375°, about 35 minutes. Uncover the last 15 minutes to brown and crisp. To make a sauce to serve with it, beat the egg yolk and sugar together and fold in whipped cream. Flavor with vanilla. Serve pudding warm but not hot. SERVES 4–5.

LEMON CRUMB PUDDING

2 cups bread crumbs made from stale but not dry bread	1 egg well beaten
	¼ teaspoon salt
	¼ cup sugar
2 cups milk scalded	¼ cup grated coconut
grated rind of 1 lemon	jam or jelly
3 tablespoons lemon juice	2 egg whites
2 tablespoons melted butter or margarine	4 tablespoons confectioners' sugar

Combine hot milk and bread crumbs and let stand 10–15 minutes. Beat well and add lemon rind and juice, melted fat, egg, salt, sugar, and coconut. Pour in greased casserole, set in pan of hot water, and bake about 30 minutes in slow oven, 300°. Remove from oven and spread with layer of almost any jam or jelly. Make meringue by beating egg whites with confectioners' sugar until stiff, spread over pudding, and return to oven for about 15 minutes, or until meringue is golden brown.   SERVES 6.

ROYAL BREAD PUDDING

1 *cup crumbs made from
stale but not dry bread*
2 *cups warm milk*
2 *tablespoons butter or
margarine*
2 *large or 3 small eggs
separated*

⅓ *cup granulated sugar*
¼ *teaspoon salt*
1 *tablespoon brandy* (*opt.*)
*currant jelly or strawberry
jam*
4 *tablespoons confectioners'
sugar*

Melt butter in milk and stir in bread crumbs. Beat egg
yolks until thick and lemon-colored, and then beat in sugar
and salt. Stir in milk and crumb mixture and brandy and
pour in greased 6-cup casserole. Set in pan of hot water
and bake in moderate oven, 350°, 35–40 minutes, or until
knife inserted in center comes out almost clean. Remove
pudding from oven and spread with a ¼-inch layer of currant jelly or strawberry jam. Make a meringue of egg
whites and confectioners' sugar, beating until they are stiff
but not dry. Spread over pudding and return to oven for
about 15 minutes, or until delicately browned. Serve either
warm or cold.   SERVES 6.

FRESH FRUIT TRIFLE

2–3 *cups coarse crumbs of
stale cake* (*plain*)
2 *oranges peeled and sliced*
¼ *pound seedless grapes cut
in two*

1 *package Vanilla Pudding*
1 *teaspoon vanilla*
½–¾ *cup cream whipped*

This is a simple and delicious dessert to make out of stale
cake. It can also be made with a "store" sponge cake, sliced
into thin layers.

Make layers of cake crumbs, orange slices, and cut
grapes. Make the Vanilla Pudding according to the directions on the package (or make a thin custard), and add

the vanilla to it. Pour over the cake and fruit mixture, poking it a number of times with a fork to be sure the custard gets all through. Chill for several hours or overnight. Top with whipped cream before serving.   SERVES 5–6.

Note: A simple thin custard is made by cooking in a double boiler, over boiling water, 2 well-beaten eggs blended with 1 pint of hot milk and 2 tablespoons sugar. A tablespoon of brandy can also be added. Stir constantly until custard is the consistency of thick cream.

JAMAICA TRIFLE

2–3 *cups ¾-inch cubes of*   ¾ *cup rum*
    stale cake (plain)   ¾ *cup mixed candied fruits*
1 *package Vanilla Pudding*   *chopped medium fine*
2 *eggs well beaten*   ½–¾ *cup cream whipped*
1 *teaspoon vanilla*

This dessert can also be made with a "store" sponge cake, which should then be sliced in half lengthwise.

Make the Vanilla Pudding according to directions on the package (or make a thin custard by your favorite recipe, and add eggs and vanilla to it. A simple custard sauce is given in the preceding recipe.)

In a glass bowl make layers of cake cubes and candied fruits, sprinkling rum well over each layer, as evenly as possible. Pour pudding over each layer, saving most of the pudding and some of the candied fruit for the top. Chill several hours or overnight. Cover with whipped cream before serving.   SERVES 5–6.

CHOCOLATE ANGEL PIE

Meringue
3 *egg whites*
pinch of salt
⅛ *teaspoon cream of tartar*
¾ *cup sifted sugar*
1 *teaspoon vanilla*
¾ *cup finely chopped nuts*
   (opt.)

Filling
4 *ounces sweet chocolate*
3 *tablespoons strong black*
   coffee
1 *teaspoon vanilla*
1 *cup heavy cream*
   whipped

Make the meringue as in the preceding recipe (notice that more sugar is required when the meringue makes the pie base). Fold in nuts last and turn out gently into a well-buttered 9-inch pie plate. With a tablespoon shape the mixture into a shallow shell, building the edges up above the rim of the dish. Bake 55–60 minutes in a very slow oven, 225°. Cool. Melt chocolate and coffee in a saucepan over hot water, cool, and stir in vanilla. Fold this mixture into the whipped cream and pour into the hollow of the meringue shell. Chill two hours before serving. SERVES 6–8.

PECAN KISSES

2 *egg whites beaten until*
   stiff but not dry
1½ *cups brown sugar*

2 *cups chopped pecan*
   meats

Sieve the sugar to be sure that it is free from lumps. Add it to the beaten egg whites, a little at a time, beating well after each addition. Fold in pecans. Drop by teaspoonfuls on well-greased cookie sheet and bake 10–15 minutes at 325°, or until delicately browned. Cool before removing with a spatula.

INDEX

Note: All leftover ingredients are indexed separately, and under them the recipes in which they appear.

DOLPHIN BOOKS AND DOLPHIN MASTERS

The bold face M indicates a Dolphin Master. Dolphin Masters are Dolphin Books in the editions of greatest importance to the teacher and student. In selecting the Dolphin Masters, the editors have taken particular pains to choose copies of the most significant edition (usually the first) by obtaining original books or their facsimiles or by having reproductions made of library copies of particularly rare editions. Facsimiles of original title pages and other appropriate material from the first edition are included in many Masters.

FICTION

ESSAYS AND LETTERS

MYSTERY

MISCELLANEOUS

DOLPHIN REFERENCE SERIES

MAGIC WITH LEFTOVERS

Lousene Rousseau Brunner

Many are the thrifty cooks who find themselves with a refrigerator full of odds and ends from previous meals. This cookbook shows how to make over 300 gourmet dishes with your leftovers, and how to save time and work by making the basic cooking for one meal stretch over several meals.

These inviting recipes have grown out of the author's own experience in creating delicious new dishes from leftover meats, poultry, fish, vegetables, and other foods. They cover a wide variety of dishes, including:

canapés	main dishes
appetizers	salads
soups	vegetables
sandwiches	desserts

Carefully indexed and clearly arranged by principal leftover ingredient, this book is an essential companion for every housewife, whether she cooks for a large family or just for two.

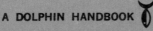

A DOLPHIN HANDBOOK

Cover design by Jack Wofgang Beck
Cover drawing by Alan Cober